Liz Jazwiec's First Award-Winning Book: A Treat You Don't Want to Miss!

American Journal of Nursing's 2010 Book of the Year

LVNtoRN.net Must-Read Nursing Book for 2012

Yes, you *can* create a positive workforce in negative times, says strategist and author Liz Jazwiec, RN. But first you have to get real about how tough a job in healthcare really is—and about the negative things you and staff members do to make it even tougher.

In the award-winning *Eat That Cookie!: How Workplace Positivity Pays Off... For Individuals, Teams and Organizations*, Liz does just that. In her darkly humorous, ever-so-slightly sarcastic style, the former ER nurse builds a case for the powerful benefits of a positive workplace. Readers will learn:

- Why hokeyness—i.e., smiley face cookies and no-negativity days—actually works
- How to decree and enforce "mandatory fun" so that it's really, well, *fun*
- How not to succumb to "process paralysis"
- Why victim-thinking is so destructive, and how to eliminate it from the organization
- How to stop judging shoe-heel smashers, pants unzippers, and other irritating patients

Put the tips in *Eat That Cookie!* into practice and you'll be amazed by the rapid improvements you see—in terms of energy, focus, productivity, and yes, happiness.

To order *Eat That Cookie!* at a special bulk discount rate, please visit www.firestarterpublishing.com or call 866-354-3473.

How *Eat That Cookie!* Is Making Healthcare Just a Bit Sweeter

Liz Jazwiec's first book, *Eat That Cookie!*, was a huge success. It was selected as the *American Journal of Nursing's* 2010 Book of the Year and as an LVNtoRN.net (Licensed Practical Nurse to Registered Nurse Programs) Must-Read Nursing Book for 2012. Loved by readers across many industries, the book was especially well received in healthcare. In fact, many of the book's readers couldn't wait to share directly with Liz just how beneficial her book was for them.

Read on to learn how *Eat That Cookie!* readers have put Liz's funny, straightforward advice to good use at their organizations, and you just might find some creative ideas for using *Hey Cupcake!* at yours!

"Providing a copy of Liz's first book, *Eat That Cookie!*, to all associates was part of our strategy to improve workplace culture. The book has empowered the entire organization to create an environment where associates at every level can manage morale, drive out negativity, and generate a work atmosphere that is positive, happy, and even fun. Her books are a must-read from the top down in every healthcare organization."

—Theodore J. Badger, Jr., FACHE
CEO, Beauregard Memorial Hospital

"We planned two full days of training around the principles in her book *Eat That Cookie!*. Liz masterfully used humor and personal stories to influence change in perspective and behavior within leaders that resulted in real impact in performance and outcomes. In fact, the book is such a sought-after item that we use it as a prize for our blog winners!"

—Robin K. Brown, RN, BSN, MHA
Director, Sentara Leadership Institute

"Used the book with my ED staff to help foster teamwork and cooperation. Shared a dozen copies between 60 nurses and everyone had a great time laughing about the humorous and anecdotal ways Liz described our daily work and relationships. Team building is a challenge for all managers; Liz helped us put things in perspective and appreciate each other for the qualities that make us all great nurses!"

—David J. O'Brien, MSN, MHA, RN
Director of Clinical Services, New York-Presbyterian/Allen Hospital

---

"At St. Mary Mercy Hospital in Livonia, Michigan, we have used the book *Eat That Cookie!* in a variety of ways. Gave copies to staff for: Nurses Week programs, orientation, shared governance council, staff members working on setting behavior standards...the list goes on for the multitude of ways you can use her book. The comment often used when leaders or staff run across someone who is challenged with change or being resistive is we need to tell them to just eat that cookie!"

—Donna Gray, MSN, BSN, RN, NEA-BC
VP of Patient Care Services, CNO, St. Mary Mercy Hospital

"Through *Eat That Cookie!* Liz's insight, humor, and stories of how healthcare functions in real life hit home with our home care agency owners, and her book has been reread many times to learn her secrets to success."

—Kathleen Gilmartin
President & CEO, Interim HealthCare Inc.

"*Eat That Cookie!* taught us we must seize every opportunity to manage those things that are in our control—most importantly our attitudes and reactions towards others. Liz's message is timeless and relevant and serves as a lasting reminder that now, more than any other time in our industry's history, our customers' perceptions of the level of service we provide matter as much as the quality of service we provide. We use her book to provide a playful yet meaningful way to facilitate serious conversations about customer service."

—Jeffrey Novorr, MHA
Assistant VP of Patient Support Services and Performance Excellence
MedStar Georgetown University Hospital

"Each attendee received an autographed copy of *Eat That Cookie!* as a memento of the most talked about leadership presentation CVHP has ever hosted. Capitalizing on the ripple effect, leaders used their *Eat That Cookie!* books as the centerpiece for front-line leader discussions within their departments. As a result, our organization has a deeper understanding of the profound connection between patient satisfaction and employee engagement."

—Robert H. Curry
President & CEO, Citrus Valley Health Partners

—Lisa A. Foust
Senior VP of Human Resources, Citrus Valley Health Partners

"Our leadership team has enjoyed learning from Liz. Often while we strategize and problem solve, someone will say, 'WWLS' (What Would Liz Say!) or, 'WWLD' (What Would Liz Do!). We pull Liz's book out—it's never too far away—and remind ourselves of that honest approach to creating a positive workplace. We refocus our energy and just 'Eat That Cookie'...we love desserts!"

—Mary Fuhro, RN, JD
VP of Patient Care Services, Newark Beth Israel Medical Center

---

"*Eat That Cookie!* is a 'must-have' roadmap to improving the patient experience. Liz's insight and use of humor resonates with all healthcare leaders, and I can't wait to read *Hey Cupcake!*"

—Lynn D. Charbonneau, Patient Experience Leader

Hey Cupcake!

We Are ALL Leaders

Liz Jazwiec

Published by:
Fire Starter Publishing
913 Gulf Breeze Parkway, Suite 6
Gulf Breeze, FL 32561
Phone: 850-934-1099
Fax: 850-934-1384
www.firestarterpublishing.com

ISBN: 978-0-9828503-4-3

Library of Congress Control Number: 2012943535

Printed in the United States of America

I dedicate this book to:

The great leaders who have inspired me, the wonderful teams I have had the privilege of leading, and to all of you out there doing the extraordinary work of leading teams.

My Leaders

Quint Studer, who has been my leader, my mentor, and my dear friend for many years. I have learned so much from him about what it truly means to have the privilege to lead. He has shown me through his own example that true leadership is about the growth and development of people.

Mark Clement, who taught me through "tough love" that being a great leader is about getting results while maintaining your integrity. Mark is an incredible leader with great integrity, and I couldn't have asked for a better example to be set for me.

Coletta Neuens, who had the courage to put me in my very first leadership role, and, in doing so, helped me to achieve so many wonderful things in my career.

My Teams

The staff of the ED at Christ Hospital 1982-1988. May God forever bless you for putting up with such a "green" leader. I will forever be in your debt for holding my hand as I navigated the early days of leadership.

The staff of the ED at Holy Cross Hospital 1991-1997. Without you, there is not a first book, a second book, presentations, or speeches. Thank you so much for rallying for me even after I had tried to give up. You never let me give up, and I am eternally grateful.

All Leaders

I am grateful for the opportunity to meet you along my travels. Whether you ask me a question after a presentation or I spend time coaching you as an individual, I very much appreciate the opportunity to advise you and strategize with you. When you ask, I learn and grow. Thank you for blessing me with the incredible fortune of being able to interact with the best leaders in the country.

Table of Contents

Foreword

We live in exciting times. Both the pace and the complexity of the workplace have been ramped up. So have the number of opportunities and challenges we face. In healthcare, the Patient Protection and Affordable Care Act is forcing change like never before. And globalization and economic pressures make it critical that organizations in all industries execute quickly and effectively.

This has huge implications for the way we work. One of the biggest changes I've seen is the role of the employee. More and more, rather than waiting for direction from a traditional leader, employees are expected to take on a leadership role themselves.

Today's employees need to be empowered to make decisions. They need to innovate on the spot to solve tough problems. They need to form strong relationships with colleagues and clients. They need to continually find ways to work effectively and efficiently at a time when every productive second counts.

As companies get flatter and more entrepreneurial, top-down leadership just doesn't work the way it once did. The old definition of who a leader is (and is not) no longer makes sense. We're *all* leaders. Lead a project, lead a committee, lead a team— it doesn't matter: It's all leadership. And we all need to have the basic tools of leadership in our own personal toolkits to call upon when we need them.

(To paraphrase the old song, everybody leads somebody sometimes!)

We hear a lot about employee engagement these days—in fact, it's the subject of my own book *The Great Employee Handbook*—and I think it means pretty much the same thing. Engaged employees are employees who are so competent and so aligned with the company's mission that they're comfortable taking on a leadership role when needed.

When we make an effort to create an organization full of engaged employees—when we inspire them with a sense of purpose, provide a strong sense of the *why* behind what we're asking them to do, and give them the opportunity, encouragement, and freedom to make mistakes and learn from them—we're *also* creating leaders.

No one gets this better than Liz.

She understands that everyone in an organization is a leader on some level because she has been there. She became a leader when she was fresh out of nursing school and, like most people who have leadership thrust upon them, had to learn the ropes as she went along. It was rewarding to watch her grow in effectiveness and confidence.

Despite any mistakes she may have made over the years—and we all do make them—the teams she led always loved and responded to her no-nonsense style, her honesty, and her sense of humor.

Finally, Liz understands that we all have a human responsibility to do our best possible work. This is obviously true in healthcare, where human lives are at stake, but organizations in *all* industries serve others in their own way. (If they don't, they won't be in business long.) And while it's couched inside Liz's humorous, slightly sarcastic voice, that message comes through on every page.

This is a great book for leaders (both official and unofficial) at every level. Like *Eat That Cookie!* before it, *Hey Cupcake!* is short and sweet. It's just the right size for busy individuals to read over a few lunch breaks—but packed with enough insight and character to boost careers and change the way we look at what it means to lead others.

Quint Studer

"If your actions inspire others to dream more, learn more, do more, and become more, you are a leader."

—John Quincy Adams

Introduction

Leaders aren't always who you think they are. And leadership is not just for the "presidents," "CEOs," and "directors" of the world. At some point, we'll all be called upon to be a "leader." (And yep, by "we" I mean "you"!) Maybe you'll be called to lead a project or a large organization. You might become the head of your shift or department. Or you might lead a committee or even an entire sales region for your company.

You get the idea. The point is you'll be called to lead and lead you shall—no matter how unprepared you think you are.

My mentor Quint Studer has said that leaders are not born, they are surprised—and that was very much the case with me. I started my career in the Emergency Department as a nurse's aide. (Don't laugh! That's what they called us back in prehistoric times.) Anyway, I had worked in this particular

ED when I was a student nurse, and when I graduated, I was very grateful to get a job there.

In fact, I was so excited to start work that when I graduated in December, I started as soon as I possibly could—December 20th. Yep, December 20th! (As it turned out I worked every single holiday that year, and I was happy about it…oh, to be young again!)

Anyway, come the following September, our head nurse stepped down. She was going on maternity leave, and when she returned, she would be working only part-time. There were four other women on the day shift who had done the same thing. Not long after she stepped down, I found myself sitting in the director's office. She asked me, in all seriousness, "Would you like the position of head nurse?"

"What?" I practically shouted. I had to stifle the urge to look back over my shoulder. Surely, someone must have come into the room behind me. Someone, perhaps, who had more than *nine months* of nursing experience under her belt. She couldn't possibly be asking me. I leaned forward and kind of choked out, "Me?"

"Yes," she said. "I know you are a new nurse…" (*NEW?!? I PRACTICALLY JUST GRADUATED!* I wanted to yell) "…but with your time with us as an aide, you've really been here three, almost four, years. You know the department well." (*BUT I'VE NEVER EVEN BEEN IN CHARGE OF ONE SINGLE SHIFT!* I had to keep myself from screaming.)

"And," she went on, "You do have your BSN."

Ah ha! That must be it, I thought. Well, that and the fact that I was just a newlywed. She must have thought she could get a year or two out of me before I, too, joined the part-time ranks.

But despite my surprise, being young, naïve, and oblivious to what was ahead of me, I said I'd do it. And just like that I went from brand-new nurse to head nurse. And yes, it was a baptism of fire.

In the beginning, it seemed like I was learning a lesson every second. And yes, one of the first was that every nurse on my team knew more than me. They were better technically, more experienced, and far greater clinicians. Another was that I had better not let my own inexperience get in the way of their delivering great care.

I remember one time when a nurse was telling me about a problem she had with a "Cabbage" patient. I listened intently and in the most comforting way I could said, "Susan, I know it is difficult dealing with an unresponsive patient, but just remember that you can reach them in other ways."

How about that for a supportive leader! I was quite impressed with my young self. Susan, on the other hand, not so much. She looked at me with the disdain of a nurse who had been in the ED longer than I had been alive.

"What are you talking about?" she snarled at me.

"Your patient who is unresponsive," I said. (I did not want to repeat the insensitive reference to a "vegetable" that she had used.)

"I don't have an unresponsive patient," she snapped.

"You said you were caring for a cabbage," I whispered, not wanting to offend anyone within ear shot.

She looked at me as if I was the dumbest nurse to carry a license. "Coronary Artery Bypass Graft…CABG…did you ever hear of that?!?" she harrumphed.

I tried to recover some of my dignity. "Oh yeah, of course! So sorry."

Susan turned away from me to go find a "real" nurse to help her.

I slid off to my office and vowed to never pretend to know more than I actually did. Tough lesson for me, although it does make for a great story today, and, ultimately, it's one of the events that helped me realize my role was making sure great nurses like Susan had what they needed—especially when I, personally, couldn't give it to them.

Several years later, I would learn this approach is called "servant leadership." At the time, though, I think I would have called it "winging it." I was very young, inexperienced, and really hadn't been given any training to help me prepare for the role. Heck, I just wanted to get through the day without being found out!

Here's one of the first things I discovered about being a leader: People aren't born with some magical leadership gene. Leaders are ordinary people doing extraordinary things.

So many people start their formal leadership positions just as I did—nurse one day, head nurse the next; pharmacist one day, director the next; administrative assistant one day, office manager the next—but the extraordinary thing is that most people rise to the occasion. They step up. They accept the responsibility. They take on the role knowing they may not be ready, and *that*, my dear Cupcakes, *is* extraordinary.

Cupcakes, what? You're probably wondering why I'm calling you Cupcakes. Well, first off, "Hey Cupcake," is a slightly cynical term of endearment, which is the best kind, in my opinion. Secondly, as much as I love cookies (as seen in my first book, *Eat That Cookie!*), I thought why not choose another beloved treat for my new book, and this time we'll talk about leadership. Besides, what workplace doesn't love even more sweets! Also, it kind of sets me up for the final title in what I'm hoping is a trilogy…something with the word "pie" maybe! And finally, a cream puff just wouldn't have looked as good on the cover!

Honestly, though, the REAL reason why I went with *Hey Cupcake!* is because I believe many of us in leadership roles are a little too soft, a little bit too sweet, and a tad bit fragile at times. I want to encourage those who find themselves in leadership roles (especially those who never expected to be there) to be less delicate. Let's toughen up, become more resilient, and bring out that convincing, formidable leader I KNOW exists in all of you.

My dear friend Father George Hazler once said, "Investing in leaders helps employees recognize their own gifts." When we are better leaders, we are better able to help our teams understand their talents and abilities.

That means if we are leading a committee, we can do a better job at bringing out everyone's thoughts and ideas. If we are in charge of a shift, it means we can help our team work more cohesively. And if we are in charge of the whole darn place, it means we have the opportunity to help everyone working there bring their very best and shine every day. See, that's what leading really is: showing those you lead how to be their very best.

Rich Bluni, author of the book *Inspired Nurse*, says it best: "If you inspire hope, then you are a leader."

Isn't that extraordinary? Think about the leaders in your life whom you've liked the best. Isn't hope one of the things they provided? Great leaders make us feel uplifted and proud, and when you feel those things, you think about what else you can accomplish and what you can help your organization become. Think about the great things that would happen if hope, pride, dignity, and joy were the backbone of most workplaces today.

In my first book, *Eat That Cookie!*, I talked about the dangers and risks of workplace negativity. I think it was so well received because everyone has experienced what it's like to work in a negative environment. (Heck, too many of us may be experiencing it right now.)

Hey Cupcake! is not a manual. It is not a handbook or a special guide. There are already tons of great books out there fitting those descriptions written for leaders. I hope that *Hey Cupcake!* becomes for leaders what *Eat That Cookie!* was for individuals, a wake-up call to move beyond what holds us back and get on with making work better.

Because no matter who you are, where you work, what you do, who you work with—you, Cupcake, are a leader. And to save you from wanting to turn right around and run out the door as I did when I suddenly became head nurse what feels like so many, many, many, many years ago, I want to share with you some of the things I've learned as a leader.

A lot of these lessons came too late in my career, so I hope you're finding them at a time when you can really put them to good use. I'll help you squash victim-thinking, end the We vs. They mentality, share some tips for dealing with the people who push your buttons, and much more. And I'll try to share my thoughts in a non-preachy (and hopefully entertaining) way.

I truly believe that we are *all* leaders. We all inspire others, or at least we can. I hope my advice and the advice I've picked up from others along the way will make it easier for you as you lead your shift, department, or organization.

Formal or informal, lifelong or temporary, I know that the people I have been fortunate enough to meet throughout my career are most definitely leaders. And if you're reading this book right now, you're one too. You all inspire me to be a better me. I hope *Hey Cupcake!* will do the same for you.

Get *Over* It! Moving Beyond "Pink Robe Rage" and Broken Cookies

Cupcakes, we're going to kick off this book by putting our best foot forward. And the absolute first step to doing that as a leader is to declare victim-thinking DOA.

(By the way, I'm qualified to talk about this subject because I am an ex-professional victim. Read my first book, *Eat That Cookie!*, to learn more about my story. In fact, Chapter 2 of that book was all about declaring victim-thinking DOA, and it was pretty darn popular with readers. *All* the chapters that dealt with this subject were well received—not only because it's a common leadership challenge but because victim-thinking makes it really hard to make room for the good.)

So, anyway, I'm starting *this* book with chapters on getting over it and letting go because being able to do both things provides the foundation for being not only a happy person, but also a great leader. First we'll look at what it takes to move past the aggravating things that can happen in the workplace. Primarily, it takes a wise leader capable of helping their teams and themselves get over it and let go of the bad. Then, in the next chapter, we will move on to letting go.

What's the difference? you may ask. Well, it's not simple, but getting over it is about moving a team past injustices or aggravations. Letting go is more about getting individuals (and yes that includes us leaders too!) to free themselves from the things that hold us back. Once we learn to do both—get over it and let go—then and only then can we let in the good.

So let me hit you with some tough love right off the bat: Get. *Over.* It! As leaders, I think we often underestimate how much our own victim-thinking rubs off on our team members. When we hold onto the bad stuff, it has a double impact in the workplace. Sure, it makes us more negative…but then our negativity makes our team members negative, too. Eventually, everyone has a death grip on every single bad thing that happens every day.

And yes, victim-thinking at the leader level is the most dangerous of all, because as Quint Studer taught me, *You cannot take your team farther than you have taken yourself.* How does victim-thinking manifest itself at the leadership level? Oh, let me count the ways. Leaders believe they can't get results. Leaders are certain their work is more difficult than everyone else's. Leaders feel the whole world is out to get them. Leaders hold onto, rehash, and ruminate on mistakes or failures…forever!

And to show you that I'm a team player, here's how I know exactly what it's like caving in to all of these aspects of victim-thinking:

In 1986 (25 years ago, can you believe it?), I was the director of the Emergency Department at Christ Hospital in Oak Lawn, IL. One day a woman suffered a cardiac arrest at home. Fortunately, a quick-thinking neighbor knew how to perform CPR correctly. The paramedics arrived and were able to get her heart rate back. She regained consciousness while in our Emergency Department and went home six days later.

It was a great save for all of us. To survive a cardiac arrest, a chain of events has to happen in exactly the right way, and sadly they rarely do. But on that day they did. Most of us working there then had never witnessed such a wonderful recovery. And we were all proud of what we'd done for this patient.

We were all feeling great until the day she went home. That day, as director of the department, I had to meet with the lady's son because he was upset with our services. Apparently during all of the chaos on the day she'd been brought in, we had lost his mother's favorite pink robe. He chastised my team for being so careless and thoughtless. (I am not making this up.)

It took every bone in my body not to look at him and say, "How inconsiderate of us! You are right. We were misguided. We *should* have been much more concerned about saving that *pink robe* instead of YOUR MOTHER!"

To this day, I still get upset when I think about my conversation with that patient's son. It's been over 25 years and I can still feel the rage along with all the sarcastic barbs I so desperately wanted to say to him.

You know what's so bad about this story? In 1986, we saw just over 50,000 patients in the ED at Christ Hospital. And as I write this story in 2012, the Missing Pink Robe Lady is the only patient I remember from that year. And I don't associate the memory with the positive work we did to keep the woman alive. I associate it with how angry I was at the son.

What's worse is that I used that situation to create fictional problems in my head in patient interactions that came later on. When patients would say nice things to me, I would think to myself, *Sure, you're happy now, but what will you be saying tomorrow? Are you going to come back and complain about a missing SOCK?!?*

That mentality wasn't good for me, and it certainly wasn't good for those in my department. You see, I didn't keep my irritation with Missing Pink Robe Lady's son to myself. No indeed! I griped about him. I made snide remarks. I led an entire chorus of cynicism when I should have gotten in one good verbal jab (hey, I'm only human!) and then moved on with my life…and allowed my coworkers to move on with theirs.

As leaders, we have to go first in getting over the bad. Sure, bad things will happen, but we have to be able to guide our team's way of looking at them.

If we focus only on the bad, it negatively colors our environment. We see only what is wrong in our work environment instead of all those things that are right. And when we do that we might as well hand out mud-colored glasses (is that the opposite of rose-colored glasses?) to our entire team.

The crazy thing is it's not even that hard to coach people to let go of the bad and get over it. It is just that as leaders, many of us think that in order to be sympathetic to our team members we must agree with and endorse the staff's negative feelings.

Don't do it! It is your job as a leader to direct your team's focus away from the bad and onto better things! (Yes, even if you secretly agree with them 100 percent!)

I learned how to focus people on the positive from my niece Lauren.

When Lauren was about two years old, I had the pleasure of babysitting her while her parents escaped for some toddler-free time. My husband, Frank, and I were never able to have children so we were very committed to being the "fun" uncle and aunt. As you're about to see, we were also very unfamiliar with the workings of a two-year-old's mind.

About halfway into our "fun" afternoon, Ms. Lauren asked me for a cookie. We had a couple of different choices, but she had her heart set on Chips Ahoy. As I handed her the cookie, I noticed it was the last one in the bag.

Lauren looked up at me with the cookie in her hand and said, "Utter han." I looked at her blankly, and she repeated, "Utter han, utter han, UTTER HAN!" Finally, I realized she wanted a cookie for her other hand. Apparently she was going through a phase in which she craved balance and symmetry…or something like that.

I showed her the empty bag thinking that that would clear things up for her. Empty bag = no more cookies. No such luck. She looked up at me and grumbled, "Utter han," and then erupted into a tantrum. But no worries, this two-year-old would not get the best of me! I devised an immediate plan. I took the cookie from her and simply cracked it in half. Then I placed each half in a hand.

Lauren looked up at me like I was a serial killer. "BROKEN! BROKEN! BROKEN! FIX IT! FIX IT! FIX IT! BROKEN! FIX IT!" she screamed. At this point, she became inconsolable. As it turned out, having a broken cookie was far worse than not having one for each hand.

In the back of my mind, I started to recall my developmental pediatric nursing course, which had described the various stages of childhood. Around two years of age, I remembered, most children have issues with wholeness. This thought gave me an idea and a glimmer of hope!

I took the cookie from Lauren's hand and tried to show her that the two halves couldn't be rejoined. But that did not stop her from chanting, "BROKEN! FIX IT! BROKEN! FIX IT," like she was an angry protester. I started hysterically laughing, which only made things worse.

Finally, I looked around the kitchen and saw a bag of pretzels. *Bag* being key here. It was full of pretzels. Forget having one for each hand, my darling niece could put one on each finger and every toe if she so chose. I traded her the broken cookie for something better—an entire bag of pretzels—and soon she was happy. The broken cookie was quickly forgotten.

Now, I understand that what we face in the workplace is not as simple as switching out cookies for pretzels.

But what we *can* do is recognize when something is frustrating or maddening for our team and then coach past it.

Move them from the negativity of the broken cookie to the positivity of the pretzels, so to speak.

When the patient's son complained about her missing robe, it would have been helpful for me if my own leader had helped me acknowledge my frustration and then had gently directed my mindset down a more positive path. Perhaps my leader at the time could have had those of us involved with the patient talk about why the son was upset about the robe and how that made us feel. It didn't need to be a long talk, just 10 minutes to get it out of our systems and gain perspective.

Then, we could have moved to the "get over it" phase by focusing on a more positive aspect of the event. For example, we could have all acknowledged the lifesaving neighbor with a note or card, signed by our entire team. We could have shared a box of doughnuts with the paramedics and staff who had been on duty the day she was brought in.

So to sum it up for you, here's how to help your team (and you!) get over it when you slide into victim-thinking. Assess why you reacted the way you did. Talk about what happened and how it made everyone feel. Let this be a time of total honesty for your team. If they want to wallow for just a second, let them wallow, but then get them back on track.

Hey, we're all human. Most of us are drawn toward negativity like a toddler to cookies or maybe an office worker to cupcakes. But too many cookies and cupcakes are bad for anyone. That's why moving your team out of victim-thinking is one of the best gifts you can give them. By helping them "get over it," you free them up to be able to appreciate everything positive in the world…and there really is plenty there to appreciate!

2

Let It Go or Go Bananas: Monkey Lessons in Releasing What's Holding You Back

You can't turn around at a leadership conference (or the business section of a bookstore) without running into an expert (or book) droning on and on about dealing with change. We get it, folks. Change is important and change is hard. But what isn't addressed enough, in my humble opinion, is the opposite of change—holding on.

Clinging to, clawing on, and just flat-out refusing to let go of things that are in the past means those things end up haunting us like ghosts every day at work. Refusing to let go holds us hostage and keeps us from moving on to where we need to be.

> As a leader, you have to be able to help your team let go of those things that are holding them back. And you have to be able to recognize when *you* aren't letting go.

My own awakening about letting go originated in kind of an unusual place—the monkey-infested streets of India. No, your eyes aren't playing tricks on you. I am now writing about monkeys and it is relevant, so swing along with me. (Get it? Swing along? Monkeys?)

Several years ago, I was at a conference where a speaker shared a story about how monkeys are captured in India. It was fascinating. He explained that in India they hold all animals in reverence. (Of course, I knew that followers of Hinduism believe cows are sacred, but I didn't know this carried over to other species.) They won't harm or hurt any animals, but apparently, there are some pretty crazy monkeys over there. These monkeys go into populated areas and take people's food, swipe ladies' purses, and just generally wreak havoc.

There is a need, especially in the big cities, to get these monkeys off the streets so that they aren't constantly harassing people. But the authorities must do so without harming them or killing them. To that end, a clever plan was devised to create a humane way to capture the monkeys and move them out of the cities and back into the wild.

How'd they do it? With bananas, of course! The speaker told us that these monkey catchers would tie a banana to a tree, and then put a hollowed out coconut shell on part of the banana. A monkey would approach the tree, put his little paw through the coconut and grab the banana. But the horizontal shape of the banana coupled with the coconut and the twine prevented the monkey from being able to make off with it.

But the monkey really wanted that banana. So while he was standing there trying to devise his own plan to get the heck out of there with his snack, the humane monkey catchers would come and drop a net on him.

Now, mind you, the monkey was never really trapped. At any point, he could have just let go of the banana and hopped away to freedom. But these monkeys never did that. Time after time, they just stood there, clutching their bananas, not really trapped, but captured anyway because they wouldn't let go.

As I sat there laughing about those silly monkeys, who were just too stubborn to let go, SHAZAM! It hit me that I was exactly like them. I was holding on to my own bananas, too many to even count probably. (Hey, at least their bananas could nourish them. Mine were only holding me back!)

Every time something happened that I thought was unfair, I would grab onto it and never let it go. Every time I predicted something wouldn't work simply because I didn't like the new program—yep, I held onto that too. Oh, and every time a boss told me something would happen but it didn't happen right away or the way I thought it should happen, there I was holding on.

I would say things like, "Remember the time they told us there wouldn't be any more staffing changes and HA, there were!" That was exactly the type of banana that I would grab and hold onto for dear life. But all along, just like the monkeys, in order to progress, in order to move forward, all I had to do was drop those bananas and walk away, but I never did. I was trapped by all those things I just couldn't let go.

Once I finally stopped whining about what happened in the past and let go of all my bananas, it was very freeing. I mean, c'mon, it's hard to hold onto all of those bananas! Sometimes I would even get mine so mixed up that I would start complaining about stuff that had never even happened. I felt like I was going bananas (pun intended)!

Holding on to old problems is a key aspect of victim-thinking. When this mindset infiltrates a team, it can suck the life right out of it. The team can't move forward because they are chasing the ghosts of past problems.

Here's a great example. One night I was out for dinner with a team of leaders from the hospital where I was working. The chief nursing officer at the time was not able to join us, which was really too bad, because in her place was the ghost of the prior CNO. It started simply enough like all good horror stories do.

We were having dinner and someone told a scary story about the previous CNO and before you knew it everyone was chiming in. All around me I heard, "Yeah, she was terrible!"; "Oh my God, she must have been the worst leader ever"; "I don't know how she ever got that job"; and so on. Then I interrupted, hoping to bring sanity back to the group. I said, "But she is gone now (You could almost hear the 'there, there' motherly tone in my voice) and remember how much you like the new CNO."

"Oh yeah, the new CNO is great," they replied in unison. But then without skipping a beat, they were back at it: "But the other one was so bad. She didn't even do Nurses Week right"; "Remember how no one ever saw her on the units?"; and "Some people thought she wasn't even a nurse!"

"...*But* she's gone now (like for 18 months!), and you like the new CNO," I gently reminded them.

"Yep, this one is great, but you just can't imagine how bad we had it here with that other one." Whine, whine, whine. "You see, Liz, one time she forgot to tell everyone about the new cardiology project and the manager of cardiology found out at a meeting."

HORRORS!, I thought. *I'm surprised you even survived to tell the tale.* "Oh and another time she..." and on and on it went.

Finally, I couldn't stand it a moment longer so I shouted, "BUT SHE'S GONE NOW AND YOU LIKE THE NEW CNO!"

They looked at me like *I* was the crazy one. "Well, yeah, we do love the new one, but there was this one time..." I gave up. Just like Freddy Krueger, it wasn't going to die.

Do you see how that team was holding on to a victim's mindset? Even after their situation had improved, they held onto the past...like those little monkeys and their bananas.

If we are going to be successful in the workplace as individuals, leaders, and colleagues, we need to learn to let things go. The only result of holding on to every single bad thing that ever happened is negativity. Whether you harbor that negativity in the hamster-wheel section of your brain—you know, the one that endlessly spins its message of resentment and self-pity—

or share it with others, it spoils what is great about *today*. I think that is really sad.

Once you drop all that negative stuff you carry with you, life gets a lot easier and a lot more fun.

Think about those leaders. Instead of celebrating the time they were spending working with a great, inspiring CNO, they complained about the past. Most likely, they missed out on opportunities to learn from the new CNO. With so much of their energy spent regurgitating the transgressions of the former CNO, I can't imagine that any of their minds were open enough to learn all they could from their new leader.

Letting go is not just for those things that happened in the distant past. Holding on for a week is too long. A day is too long. Heck, an hour is too long! Just give yourself five minutes to gripe and fume—internally, if possible, so you don't spread the negativity to everyone around you—then let it go.

Chances are you hold on to things every day. And those things keep you from being satisfied or fulfilled. Letting go means just that: letting go of all of the things that keep you upset or stuck playing the role of victim. Believe me, having worked in an ED for over 18 years, I know about the connection between an inability to let go and victim-thinking. I don't think an ED nurse coined the term "red-headed stepchild," but we sure love playing the role.

Here's the deal: Once you believe you are that ill-fated redhead, you become her! You can find reasons every day that will support your theory. The supervisor always takes too long to answer your page, *whaah!* The attending physician is curt with you on the phone, *whaah!* Purchasing forgets part of your order, *whaah! whaah!*

Just LET IT GO! Maybe your supervisor is busy, the attending physician had another phone call come through, and purchasing simply made a mistake. It doesn't matter. Just. Let. It. Go.

When we hold on to what went wrong in the past, we miss what is happening right now. We miss what is good about today. And isn't that sad?

Let go of the past. Don't get trapped holding onto something that you can't change.

Are you starting to get it? The difference between being a victim or victor, a whiner or a winner, a chimp or a champ is all in the letting go. So, c'mon, drop those bananas!!!

3

Knock, Knock, Cupcakes! How to Open the Door to Letting in the Good

There's a reason I've been talking about getting over it and letting go. Until you drop all that heavy baggage you've been carrying around you won't be able to see the good stuff that's right in front of your face.

Now, if you've devoted yourself wholeheartedly to victim-thinking, you probably don't think there even *is* anything good at your workplace. But those of us on Planet Get Over It know that when you let in the good you'll find your life overflows with compliments, thank yous, 'atta boys, and many other signs of gratitude (sometimes even cookies and cupcakes!) in the course of your workday.

Recognition is absolutely something we should all pay closer attention to at work, but really it's step two in the gratitude process.

Step one is making sure people are ready to *accept* that recognition.

As a leader, it isn't enough to walk around finding nice things to share with your team; you need to make sure that they are open to hearing recognition and letting in the good.

Those of us in healthcare have been working on recognition for many years. Some of us give out "Wow" cards that thank employees for a job well done, keep recognition logs, or even have organization-wide recognition committees. *Then, why,* some of you are probably asking, *are people still so darn negative? So whiney? Such victims? Why are they so quick to play the role of the red-headed stepchild?* Simply put, they don't know how to let in the good!

For example, let's say as a leader you recommit to recognition. You decide you're going to come bouncing into work on Monday with a new outlook. You're going to recognize your team's good work and boy are they going to appreciate it!

You start your shift, observe your team for a bit, and almost immediately, you notice Jane, one of your nurses, interacting with a patient and his family. Once she is out of the room you approach her and say, "Jane, I just saw you with that patient and you were amazing. I could see their anxiety diminish as you were talking to them. Thanks so much for all you do for our team!"

You might be thinking, *Wow, I bet Jane just loved those kind words!* Wrong! Jane didn't hear them because Jane doesn't know how to let in the good. Here's what actually happened:

Jane looked at you, rolled her eyes, and said, with all the sarcasm she could muster, "Well, I guess that's why I get paid the BIG bucks!"

Hmph, that is certainly not what you were expecting, but you are a determined leader so you don't give up. A little bit later, you go into the storeroom and you notice that Tim, a tech, has straightened the entire room and everything is neat and organized.

You go find Tim and say to him, "Tim, the storeroom looks amazing. Thank you so much for doing that. We'll be so much more efficient now because we won't have to waste so much time looking for things. You have really made a big difference today."

Tim responds by opening his arms and giving you a big hug! Thanking *you* for thanking *him*, with a big ol' smile on his face. Right?

Uh, no, not exactly. (I must have dozed off for a minute there.) Like Jane, Tim doesn't know how to let in the good either. What Tim *actually* does is shrug, and as he's already walking away from you, he mutters, "Don't get too excited. It will be a mess again before the end of the day."

Man, these people are harsh! As a leader, now you're bummed. You're also far less likely to want to do more recognition, but that is not the problem. The bigger problem is that when Jane and Tim are asked, "Do you feel appreciated at work?" they say, "No! No one ever tells me anything good around here. The only time I hear anything from my boss is when there is something wrong."

Now, I just don't think that is true! I *know* we hear good things all the time, every day. Patients say thank you. Customers express appreciation. Leaders pass out compliments. Executives praise good work. And we receive gratitude from our colleagues and our own team members. What is true is that a lot of people just lack the ability to let that good stuff in.

Why? It's really kind of simple. Most of us were never taught to accept compliments or gratitude graciously.

Sure, we're all taught, from an early age, how to accept a gift with grace. Here's what that lesson usually looks like: Imagine that it's your fifth birthday and you tear open a gift, look inside, loudly squawk, "But it's just CLOTHES!" and then toss the box and its contents aside.

You're probably going to be in big trouble. In fact, if your mom is anything like my mom, she'll probably biff you in the head and say, "Tell Grandma thank you for the present."

"But it's clothes!" you protest.

"Tell her thank you!" she'll repeat ominously, this time with a very convincing glare in her eyes and a little more emphasis. You surrender and mumble, "Thanks for the clothes, Grandma." (Gee, how sincere that sounds!)

Over the years, we learn these lessons in gracious gift acceptance very well and take them with us into adulthood. Think about all the times you've had to "fake it" in your own life. When you move into a new home and Aunt Ida visits and gives you a hideous vase as a housewarming gift, you plaster a big smile on your face and say something like, "Well, this is so very…so very…hmmm…special! We will find the perfect spot for it!"

Of course, in your honest opinion, that perfect spot is the closet. But Aunt Ida doesn't need to know that, so when she comes to visit, you pull that baby out, dust it off, and put it on the table so that she can see it on display.

So most of us did learn to graciously accept *gifts*. But what about learning how to accept compliments and gratitude— which are gifts of a different type? When I was growing up, and I'll bet this is true for a lot of you too, that lesson was somehow missing from my parents' repertoire. In fact, for me, it was the opposite.

If a teacher thanked me for helping in the class and I went home and boasted to my father, "Hey, Dad, guess what? Sister Margaret said I was the most helpful student today! I passed out the papers, collected the homework, and cleaned her boards for her. She thanked me for being so helpful!" He'd most likely ask, "Couldn't you have done more?"

My mother was worse. One day when my sister and I were about eight and ten years old, we ran up to her and asked in unison, "Mom, which one of us is prettier?" Without batting an eye, she replied, "Neither one of you would win a beauty contest." Ha! To this day, that still makes me laugh. I guess you could say that back in the '60s they weren't so worried about our self-esteem.

The point, though, is that when we reach adulthood many of us have no idea how to react in the face of compliments and gratitude. If a colleague says, "Thanks for helping with that project!" your first response is probably, "Oh, it was nothing. I wish I could have done more. I'm sorry I didn't get to all of it."

Or let's say a coworker tells you that your scarf is pretty. You reply, "This old thing? I've had it forever. It was cheap. I got it at a garage sale."

Or you bring in cookies for a potluck and a teammate asks, "Did you make those cookies in the lounge? They are sooooo good!" You reply, "Yeah, the oven kind of got away from me. They should have been a little chewier. These turned out overdone." Yikes! Are you starting to see a pattern here?

I suppose it is okay to let this kind of thing go in your personal life. I'm certainly not going to force you to start feeling good about everything you do and basking in your accomplishments. That would be crazy, right? But at work refusing to let in the good can affect your morale, and yes, that negativity will spread to others.

For example, let's say a phlebotomist goes into a room to draw blood. She does everything perfectly. When she's done, she asks the patient if there is anything else she can do. The patient says, "No, but I'm sure you hear this all the time…you have a great technique. I could hardly feel that needle!"

If the phlebotomist just says, "Okay then, bend up your arm so you don't get a bruise," two people lose out. First of all, the patient loses because her kind words were just ignored. Secondly and most importantly, the phlebotomist loses because the patient told her something lovely about her work and she just totally missed the opportunity to feel great about it.

As leaders, we have to coach our teams to let in the good.

Trust me, it won't be easy. It will be a process, but one that will be so very valuable to individual team members and your team as a whole.

Had I been coaching that phlebotomist and heard the patient say, "You must hear this all the time, but you have a great technique!" I would guide her to say, "Well, I've not heard it from you. That just made my day!"

See how that creates a much more positive experience? See how if that phlebotomist reacts to compliments like that as little as once or twice a week, it will make her outlook more positive?

It is not an easy thing to do. I mean, many of us have been turning down and ignoring compliments and gratitude for a long time. As with anything that is difficult, I recommend using humor to drive home the importance of letting in the good.

I worked with one organization in Mississippi, and they decided that whenever they thanked someone and got that "Oh, it was nothing" reply, their response would be a very stern, "You WILL accept my gratitude!"

One day, I was working with Greg Paris, the CEO of Monroe County Hospital, a great hospital in Iowa. I noticed his tie and said, "Greg, I love that tie!" He said, "Why thank you, Liz! I look forward to receiving your compliments each and every day!" Ha! We both laughed, but it worked. We both felt more positive after that interaction.

Bring this subject up at the next staff meeting. Set a goal as a department that you will all recognize one another's accomplishments and accept, wholeheartedly, the gratitude you're shown for a job well done. Hey, it may seem a bit cheesy or touchy-feely at first, but the more you practice the more natural it will feel.

Please help your teams let in the good. When they do, I think they'll realize they hear good things at work five or six times a day.

They'll hear "thank yous" from the people they serve, from leaders, from coworkers, from vendors, and on and on.

If you work in healthcare, these kudos shouldn't be hard to come by. After all, we make people feel better when they're at their most scared and vulnerable. Sometimes we even save their lives.

If you work in some other field and happen to be reading this, chances are this principle applies to you, too. You are helping someone or making someone's life better in some way. If not, you wouldn't be making money for your products and services. Just do your best work and listen for the gratitude…you'll hear it.

Leading your team to let in the good will bring them away from victim-thinking and many steps closer to feeling great about what they do. And hey, we're at work for eight hours or more a day…that's a lot of time to harvest some good, and it sure beats the alternative.

4

The Dark Side of Change: How to Drag Your Team Out of the Valley of Despair

Change. We sure hear a lot of inspirational quotes about it. And I hate to think about the trees that have died so people could print the tons of business and leadership books encouraging us to embrace it. You'd think we loved change, but nope—we don't. No one really likes it. I sure don't. (How's that for honesty?)

You're probably thinking, *But Liz, you speak about change all the time.* Yeah, I do, but that doesn't mean I have to like it. What I do understand and appreciate about change is that it's a part of life. It's how we get better.

And, my dear Cupcakes, if you are going to have a successful team, then you need to learn how to accept change, understand it, and, you guessed it, *lead* it.

The first thing we need to do is get real. Change isn't going to be fun. Not unbearable—not like natural childbirth or a week with the in-laws—but definitely uncomfortable. But how many things in life that make us better people aren't at least a little uncomfortable?

Yes, change is difficult, and it requires a certain amount of stick-to-it-tiveness that those you're leading might not have. That's why they have you. It's your job to lead them through the Valley of Despair.

What's the Valley of Despair, you may be asking? Well, if you've read any of the millions of books about change, you've probably encountered this analogy. It's supposed to represent your mentality as you go through a major change.

The Valley of Despair looks like this:

Isn't it gorgeous? If you just screamed, "No!" at the top of your lungs (or silently in your mind, if you're worried about people thinking you're crazy), you probably remember exactly what it feels like to be stuck down in the lowest point of the Valley. It sucks. You eventually came out on the other side, but when you were at the bottom, it was hard to see the sunshine and roses waiting at the end of your climb.

But because I'm not much of a theoretical thinker, I came up with my own way of thinking about the Valley of Despair. (Honestly, I've never been wild about the name. It sounds more like a '60s soap opera to me.) Instead, I teach what I call the "Clean Out the Closet Theory." For men, it might make more sense to call it the "Clean Out the Garage Theory."

Here's how it works: You decide that it's time to clean out your closet. And not just a little straightening up here and there. You're going for a total makeover. You're excited. Thoughts of clothes organized by color and on matching hangers, shoes neatly arranged in individual bins, and baskets lining the shelves dance through your head. You pick a Saturday for the closet revamp and buy all the new hangers, baskets, and bins you'll need for the big change. You lay everything out and think about how much fun it's going to be to give your closet a good old-fashioned makeover and how great it's going to look when you're done. Heck, maybe even HGTV will come a-calling!

Finally, the day of the big clean-out arrives. You wake up excited and ready to start. In fact, you don't waste a second. Almost immediately you start pulling clothes out of your closet, separating them into piles—some on the bed, some on the floor, some on the dresser. There's a pile for summer clothes, winter clothes, donations, etc. Then, you move on to shoes. You consider arranging them by pairs, but there are a lot so for now you just kneel on the floor and throw them over your shoulder to get them out of the closet. They land everywhere around the room, but you're not worried; soon everything will be organized!

As you are pulling some old boxes off of the top shelf, you realize how dusty it is up there. As much as you would like to ignore it, you know you can't put new stuff on top of a dirty shelf. And really, now that you look at it, the entire closet could use a good wipe down.

"All of this extra cleaning was not part of the plan!" you grumble. But unfortunately, now it's standing in the way of your finishing the closet so you keep going, but with a little less enthusiasm than you had when the morning began. (For those of you keeping up at home, now we've begun the slide into the Valley of Despair. And we're about to start picking up speed on our fall to the bottom.)

You pull out dust rags, spray cleaners, brooms, and dustpans. With a swish swish here and a scrub scrub there, the closet is eventually spic and span. By this time most of the morning is gone. You are getting tired, but you congratulate yourself on a job well done.

Then you make the mistake of turning around to look at the rest of the room. It is a mess. It looks like your closet just spewed its contents all over your room. There are clothes, shoes, and boxes everywhere. Meanwhile, your new closet accessories are barricaded in a corner, mocking you. You want to walk away. You want to quit or maybe even take a nap, but you can't even see the BED!

Blam! Now, all your energy is zapped. You don't even want to think about how much time and energy is going to be required to finish this project. The only thing ahead of you is a lot of hard work. (Why did you ever think this was a good idea, anyway?) For a brief moment, you consider just shoving everything back in the closet willy-nilly, but obviously you can't do that.

Guess what? You're at the bottom of the Valley of Despair—or, as I like to call it, Rock Bottom of Closet Cleaning Chaos. You take a deep breath, gather your resolve, and trudge back into the fray.

As you hang up your clothes on the new hangers, you mutter to yourself, "There was nothing wrong with the old hangers, but nooooooo, I *had* to have these new, color-coded hangers." Your idea of putting your shoes in individual shoe bins no longer seems very good. In fact, you start to find fault with the shoe bins you were in love with yesterday.

An hour or two goes by and eventually you notice that you've made some real progress. The clothing piles that had engulfed the room are now much smaller. And when you look in the closet, you get a tinge of satifaction from seeing all the clothes so neatly hung by color on their pretty new hangers. You get a burst of energy as you complete the task, and as an added bonus, you decide to nail a couple of hooks on the wall for belts and scarves.

And finally you're done! The closet is cleaned and reorganized. A great sense of accomplishment and pride sweeps over you. A couple mornings later, as you are getting dressed, you don't have to fight with your clothes to find the right shirt, or crawl on your knees, searching the back of the closet for a matching shoe. You wonder why you didn't do this sooner.

And that is my very scientific "Clean Out the Closet Theory." While it might not rival Einstein's Theory of Relativity, it does paint a picture of what it's like trying to make a change. And I think it makes the Valley of Despair image a little easier to take in.

Most attempts at real change are going to involve many ups and downs. First you decide (or, let's face it, are told) that you have to make a change. In the beginning, the change seems like a good enough idea to you. Maybe even a great idea. So when you get started, you're excited and filled with enthusiasm. But as you get going, things are a little more difficult than you expected. Still, you push forward.

As you go, implementing the change becomes even more difficult. There's pushback from your team, and the steps you thought would be easy turn out not to be. Eventually, you're exhausted and want to stop. You're at the lowest point of the Valley of Despair.

At this point, though, you realize that despite your exhaustion there really is no turning back. So you trudge forward. Slowly but surely you begin to work your way out of the Valley. You realize you and your team have gained knowledge and insight, and you're putting them to good use. Finally, you start seeing real progress. Yes! That change you've been trying so hard to implement is actually leading to great results. Your energy level surges and it suddenly gets easier to forge ahead.

Voilà! Once all is said and done, you find that things are way better than they were before and your results improve. (Hint: If you want to learn more about this, read Quint's *Straight A Leadership*. He describes it all in great detail.)

Now for a bit of bad news. As a leader, be prepared: You're going to hit the Valley of Despair much harder than those you're leading. In addition to your own anxiety associated with the change, you'll be dealing with the anxiety and despair of everyone on your team. And rest assured, they'll let you know exactly how bad they're feeling about things. (Ah, the joys of leadership!)

Your low performers will be especially vocal. They're not just venting; they're actively trying to drag your middle and high performers down. Truthfully, low performers love, love, love the Valley of Despair. It's like their home away from home. It is where they are the most comfortable, just like a troll under a bridge. During a change initiative, they can't wait to plummet right into the Valley so they can wallow in what they love most—negativity.

It's at this (low) point that most change initiatives start to tip toward failure. Instead of understanding that they're just in the most difficult stage of implementing the change, many teams think they've hit an impossible barrier, more like a brick wall. So, they quit. They give up on change. After this happens, it can be very difficult to try to attempt to change again. Employees, and maybe even the leaders themselves, will say, "That will never work here. We've tried, and it's impossible to change how we do things."

Luckily, with the right mindset, you can lead your team through the Valley of Despair.

All teams dealing with change will find themselves in the Valley at one point or another. Knowing this allows you to include steps in your overall change process to help you and your team deal with the Valley.

In the beginning, sit your team down and explain to them, "While we are on this journey, it is likely that when we're about 45-65 percent of the way through the process we will hit the Valley of Despair." If it helps, feel free to use my Clean Out the Closet Theory to help them visualize exactly what you're talking about.

Then ask the team, "What should we do when we get to this point? What should we do when we are discouraged and doubting our success?" You'll probably get some great suggestions. Over the years, I've certainly heard great ideas in response to this question. For example, one of my teams suggested that when we reached the Valley we should have one meeting to just moan and groan and write down all our complaints, issues, and difficulties. At the end of that meeting, the plan was to throw the papers into our outdoor fire pit and watch them burn. We would then vow to each other that we would come to the next meeting all recharged.

And if that doesn't work for you, then there's always Jose Cuervo. That's right. One of my teams said that when they hit the Valley they would find their friend Jose Cuervo and let him lead them out!

Whether you go tactical or tequila, it is essential that you make a plan to help ease the distress caused by the Valley of Despair.

The absolute best time to do this is in the beginning when everyone is positive, fired-up, and ready to go. Write your plan down, save it, and then when the time comes, USE it.

Unfortunately, most teams never do plan for the Valley, so when they get there they don't recognize it for what it is. As I said before, if you don't know what it is—and that it's uphill from there—when you hit it, you quit it. And that, my dear Cupcakes, is the danger. By the time you hit the Valley, you've really come too far. Don't quit now. The minute you recognize that you are in the Valley, BLAM, implement your plan.

Of course, you can't stand around burning papers or going round for round with Mr. Cuervo forever. Once you've recognized you've hit the Valley, it is time to quickly do what you need to do to deal with it and then get back to the task. This is where the leader is so vital. You must be wise enough to give your team time to wallow in the Valley and then bring them back to the task.

Remember, you are very close to completion. Remind your team that there are much better things ahead. Reiterate the vision and goal for the change. And finally, renew your own commitment to leading the team to the finale.

And that, my Cupcakes, is the Valley of Despair, summed up for those of us who can't always follow theory! We start. We are excited. The middle is excruciating. There is a burst of energy toward the end, and finally things are truly better.

All leaders need to know how to shepherd their teams through the Valley of Despair. Knowing that your team might fall into it is half the battle. The other half is having the tenacity, ability to inspire, and the drive to lead everyone out of it.

It's up to you to guide your team out of the Valley past those trolls. I promise things will be better on the other side. Once you've led your team out of the Valley, you'll have given them the greatest gifts: accomplishment, pride, success. They'll have a "closet" they want to keep revisiting and showing to others…and *their* success will be the gift you give yourself.

5

The Ugly Truth: Debunking the Buy-In and Teamwork Myths

You probably didn't know we live in a perfect world, did you? Apparently, in the world of leadership literature, we do. With perhaps just a smidge of exaggeration, I'd say their account of how to manage change goes something like this:

First, introduce the new behavior and explain why it's important. Then, watch people miraculously cast away their old way of doing things and buy in quickly and easily to new desired behaviors. Teams work together efficiently and have great respect for one another. Everything goes so well and comes so easily that leading is almost effortless. All you need to do as a leader is achieve Buy-In and Teamwork and then you can kick your feet up on your desk and relax.

SORRY, but that's not exactly how it works. Now, don't come after me with burning torches. (My running-from-angry-villagers tunic is at the dry cleaners.) I am not saying that Buy-In and Teamwork aren't important. They are very important. But most leaders have been told that they come first—that progress can't be made until you have Buy-In and Teamwork. And I think that's very misleading for leaders.

Frankly, it's unfair to set people up this way. For years, leaders have been struggling to accomplish both of these as a first step. And because that is almost always impossible, it has left many of them frustrated and feeling like failures.

Let's take some time to unravel the mysteries behind the Buy-In and Teamwork myths and get a better understanding of how these important aspects of leadership play out in the *real* world.

First of all, Buy-In and Teamwork are not strategies. They're not the way you get results; they *are* the results.

They are the consequences of a first-rate culture, or a vast change in behavior. In other words, they don't come first. They come *after* a lot of hard work.

Let's start by focusing on Buy-In. Often, people will come up to me after a presentation and say, "I loved everything you said, but how do you get your staff to Buy-In?" My answer is always the same, "I don't." Man! You should see the astounded looks on their faces. It's almost as if I've just told them that Santa Claus doesn't exist. (Even though we all know he does!)

Once their surprise wears off, I gently explain that Buy-In comes last, and that the only way to achieve Buy-In is to hold people accountable for the desired behaviors. (I believe this is so important that I devoted an entire chapter to it in my first book, *Eat That Cookie!*) Accountability is the only way to change bad behavior or reinforce great behavior.

To achieve Buy-In you must do the difficult work of holding your team to the desired actions you want them to take.

When I used to speak a lot about helping organizations implement change, I would teach an acronym that I learned from Quint. It's BARF! Okay, so that is not *exactly* the acronym that he taught to me, but I changed it up a little to suit me better. Here's how it goes:

- **Belief**
- **Action**
- **Result**
- **Faith** (Full disclosure: "Faith" was originally "Understanding," but that spelled BARU, and that is not nearly as fun as BARF!)

The lesson went like this: When implementing change, the first thing you need is the *belief* that a strategy will work. Then you need to take *action* and implement the change. The team's actions then produce *results*. And that is when most people gain a better understanding of why the change works, and their *faith* in the new way is strengthened.

To illustrate this little formula, I always like to use one of my favorite stories from my time at Holy Cross Hospital. Some of you might remember this story from *Eat That Cookie!* I used it when describing how we need to change behaviors, not attitude.

One of our first service initiatives at Holy Cross was to start saying "Hi" to everyone in the hallways. We couldn't wait for Buy-In on this one because up until this point the hallways had been a no-talking zone. You see, at one point in the dim and dusty past, the good sisters thought refusing to let us talk amongst ourselves would keep us in line! They must have mistaken us for elementary school students.

Anyway, someone came up with the idea that this no-talking policy wasn't working too well and, thankfully, decided to change it. The idea behind the change was that if we all said "Hi" to each other and to the patients, their families, the hospital's vendors, basically everybody, the hospital would have a friendlier atmosphere. This belief was shared by the leadership team, but it would prove to be difficult getting everyone else on board.

Guess what? It was far from easy changing these long-ingrained habits. The task itself, saying "Hi" in the hallways, was simple, but holding people accountable for it was where the real leadership challenge came. Those of us who were leaders had to find a way to help people commit to the new desired behavior.

So, we ended up with Hello Police. One day an officer of the HPD (Hello Police Department, get it?!?) called me from another department and told me that Karen, one of the ED nurses, was not saying hello in the hallways.

I called Karen into my office. "Will you PLEASE start saying 'Hi' in the hallways?" I asked. (I desperately wanted the hallway cops off of my back.)

"I am busy saving LIVES," Karen retorted.

"Not in the hallways you aren't!" I snapped.

By forcing this action throughout the organization, guess what, we started seeing results. In the category "Overall friendliness of the hospital," we saw a significant jump in our patient satisfaction survey scores. And it was seeing those results that helped everyone understand that the strategy worked. In other words, we gained *faith* that it was a good approach. And that, my dear Cupcakes, is the recipe (Sorry, I couldn't help myself!) for Buy-In.

It's also essential to note that Quint always emphasizes the importance of explaining the *why*. As we roll out new behaviors, our teams should know *why* we are doing it. In other words, you should share the *belief.* Why are we going to say "Hi" in the hallways? Because we (the leaders) believe it will give everyone the correct perception that we are a friendly organization, and that is very important in the healing mission of our hospital.

Once the team sees the positive results of the new behavior, your high and solid performers will most definitely have faith, understanding, and yes, the ever-lovin' Buy-In that saying "Hi" in the hallways is a good thing. (Your low performers will be more challenging. We'll address them later in the book.)

Now, let's take a look at Teamwork. The myth goes that Teamwork comes first and then all is right in the world (or at least your department). But just like Buy-In, Teamwork is a result, not a strategy for achieving other things.

Usually the biggest obstacle to achieving Teamwork is negativity.

If you have negative people on your team, you will never achieve the cooperation, collaboration, and communication you need in order for the group to work together effectively.

There is a ton of information out there telling all of us how to achieve Teamwork. Some of it is okay. Some of it is *crazy*. I remember back in the '90s there were some wacky activities that were supposed to help with teambuilding. These brilliant suggestions included running a fake lemonade stand, keeping a balloon in the air, and, my favorite, lifting your team members over a wall. Now, I'm telling you, if people were going to lift me over a wall, forget the team, you had better go and get the entire village.

Your high performers and rock-solid employees instinctively know how to work together as a team, whereas for low performers, victim-thinkers, and Debbie Downers, it doesn't come quite as easily. If you don't believe me, let's take a walk down memory lane.

Think about a day when you arrived at work ready to tackle the day. No one had called in sick. It wasn't all that busy. You thought you were in for a quiet ride. But then you looked at the schedule and saw names that told you in an instant that you were about to have the longest shift of your life. YEP, you were working with negative people—whiners, complainers, victims—who wouldn't understand Teamwork if they built a million fake lemonade stands or shoved each other up and over the Great Wall of China.

Now think back to one of your busiest, craziest days as a team member. (Maybe it was yesterday, so you don't have to think that far back!)

So you came into work and the place was wild. There were patients all over the place, or if you're not in healthcare, maybe there were work orders everywhere. You find out that you don't have any clerical support, and two people have called in sick.

You were beginning to think this was going to be the worst shift of your life, but then you looked down at the schedule. Your entire outlook brightened as you saw the list of people you would be working with. Rock-solid, every one—no whiners, no complainers, no slugs, and no Debbie Downers. And in that moment you realized everything was going to be okay, because no matter how crazy things might get, at least you knew you had your A-List players to rely on. You knew you'd be fine because those A-List players knew how to work together for the betterment of the team.

See, where negativity and victim-thinking exist, Teamwork won't happen. In earlier chapters, we've touched on how these factors can infest a workplace. As a leader, it's up to you to do the work to eliminate them, and then, you'll get that Teamwork that makes work such a pleasure. Once you eliminate negativity from your workplace, you will find that Teamwork will soar!

People will work together, achieve outcomes, and reach goals. You'll have your dream team, so to speak.

So remember, my Cupcakes, as leaders, Buy-In and Teamwork are very important to all of us, but they don't come first. They come after doing the hard work of leadership—holding people accountable, replacing negative staff with positive, and achieving success. Once these things are in place, you will find your high-performing, solid team members have bought in and are working together like a championship team.

6

They Mean Trouble: How to Handle Your Evil Queens and Wicked Poisoners

I saw a quote the other day that for some reason really resonated with me:

"I may look calm, but in my head I've killed you three times."

I have no idea where it originated. From what I can tell it's one of those anonymous quotes that finds its way to Facebook and spreads like wildfire. Everyone knows it, yet no one knows who started it. But I do know why it's caught on: It's a universal human truth that there are certain people who just inspire rage in others.

When you're a leader, such problem people can really make you crazy. Why? Not just because you don't like them personally but because they stand squarely between you and a great work environment.

Problem employees weigh everyone down. Let them infest the workplace and they'll suck the lifeblood out of any organization. They will tank your morale and lower the motivation bar for everyone. In short, they have got to go!

As a leader, properly handling (and by properly handling, yes, in most cases, I mean firing) problem employees should be one of your highest priorities.

Let them stick around too long and one day you'll look around and find that they're all you've got. That's because problem employees drive the good people out of your organization.

The primary reason people stay with or leave an organization is their coworkers and leaders. When they like their colleagues, they stay. When their colleagues make every day a chore, they leave. (Hey, life is short. Why should anyone have to be miserable at work?) High performers, in particular, resent it when troublemakers repeatedly get away with upsetting the team.

In fact, in some studies the "getting away with it" factor is what many workers cite as evidence that their leader is unfair. And the irony is that many leaders don't realize how personally their followers take it when they fail to step in and deal with problem employees.

As a leader of a clinical unit (the ED), I was shocked to find out that I had no idea how my team members measured fairness. I always thought it meant that if you worked on Thanksgiving then you would get Christmas off. Or if you had the most seniority on the night shift, then you would get the next day shift position that opened up.

But in the eyes of your best employees, that's not what fairness is at all. For them fairness means you, the leader, taking the initiative to deal with the negative folks who make their work more difficult every day.

> As a leader, I quickly learned that my first responsibility was always to my team. I had to suck it up and get good at firing people, because sometimes getting rid of a negative person was the best thing I could do for my team.

In this chapter, we'll take a look at a couple common types of problem employees and how to deal with them. I won't spend much time talking about *no performers*—those bold creatures who don't show up, specialize in sloppy work, leave without telling anyone, ignore organizational policies, and so on. For the most part, I think leaders do a good job of moving these folks out of the organization

We'll be looking at special categories of low performers. These problem employees are a little trickier because occasionally they're technically sufficient workers, but their demeanor *always* brings down the team. We used to call them people with attitude problems. We *need* to call them ex-employees. They are toxic, and no workplace can thrive with these kinds of people on board.

First up, the Evil Queens. (Yes, there can be Evil *Kings*, too!) You know the types. They act like they should be treated like royalty because they've managed to become very competent at certain aspects of the job. They are the ones who know how to figure out every computer system problem. They know how to calibrate every machine. They deliver good clinical care. In the world of nursing, Queens are commonly referred to with a disclaimer, "She's a good nurse, but…"

The Queens have everyone believing that they are the only people who care about doing a job the right way, and they make it very well known when things are less than perfect. In healthcare, Queen nurses have most of the doctors believing that if they should ever leave the hospital, the patients would never be PROPERLY cared for ever again. And of course, they deliver messages like this with the backs of their hands up to their foreheads for added effect.

Queens are dangerous because they will eat your young. They are miserable and unapproachable, and as a result, new employees are very intimidated by them. I bet Queens drive out two or three new employees within every organization every year. Do the math. They have to go!

These individuals must be made to understand that it isn't okay to point out everything that is wrong with the organization. As leaders, you have to show them that if they are not part of the solution, they ARE the problem.

In 1997, I was helping Quint at a hospital in Pensacola. One of the things I was focused on was the Emergency Department, and let me tell you there was a lot to focus on there. Things were certainly troubled. Several staff members were moved out of the organization and new people were hired. But there was still a lot of negativity due to the high number of Queens in the ED.

One day, I came into the staff lounge as the night shift was waiting to badge out. Well, this group of Queens were so evil and menacing, for a minute I thought they could have been Biker Chicks. Yep, Biker Chick Queens are especially frightening because they can have you running for cover as they spew a mix of negativity and aggressive complaining and grumbling. I knew I had to take immediate action so I asked them, "What is *so* wrong?"

The loudest one stood up, put her finger in my face, and said, "There are way too many new people working here."

Hmmm, okay. I asked, "And how do you propose we fix that, fire them? Then, we would have to hire 'new' new people."

"Well, I am tired of coming to work every night and putting my license on the line," one of them shouted. Oh brother. Here we go! For those of you who don't know, the "license on the line" is a pretty famous complaint for troublemaking nurses. Can you hear my eyes rolling from here?

So right then I left the lounge and called the Florida state licensing board and asked for a list of all the nurses in the state who had lost their licenses in the past two years. Guess what I discovered? There are really only a few ways you can lose your license, and most of them involved felonies—you know, using and selling drugs, committing murder, etc. The state licensing board assured me that training new employees was not on the list.

I shared my findings with them. I told them based on my research that if you rob a liquor store and shoot the clerk in order to get money for your crack cocaine habit you would definitely be in danger of losing your license. However, if you work a night shift with a novice, you are in the clear!

Now, occasionally, there will be a Disney-style happy ending and your Evil Queen will change her ways. But far, far too often that just isn't the case. As a leader, you must be prepared to take the necessary steps to move them out of the organization.

Know that this process will probably take a long time. In most cases, your Queens have had perfect evaluations. And in all fairness, their behavior has been tolerated…Remember, if you permit it, you promote it! So, if you are a leader, start working with your Human Resources Department right away in order to begin the process of either getting a Queen to change her behavior or moving her out of the organization.

Remember, in these situations, HR is your friend. Not the enemy. Your HR contact will likely try to save this employee, but you should be very upfront and specific about why you think they need to go. Don't just say, "Queen Mabel is trouble." And DEFINITELY don't say, "Queen Mabel has a problem." When HR folks hear that, a little voice in their heads goes off saying, "Save her! Save Mabel!"

In your first meeting with HR, you need to say, "I have a woman working in our department, Mabel Glumly. She needs to be removed from our organization." Now I guarantee you that HR will still try to save her, as they should. Remember, in a way, they act as an advocate for all of your organization's employees. But they also understand that sometimes bad employees have to go, and when you let them know why your Queen is one of them, they'll quickly get the picture.

As I've mentioned above, Queen Mabel probably has 15 years' worth of perfect evaluations. That's okay. Let HR tell you how to get started and listen to them. They will assist you in getting the right documentation, gathering the written warnings, going through the rest of the disciplinary process, and so on. In my experience, when HR is involved from the very beginning, there is a very slim chance that you will be unsuccessful in firing the individual.

If Queen Mabel has been a problem for the last 10 years, it will probably take you about a year and a half to terminate her. That's alright. Don't let that stop you. Just start where you can and begin to move forward.

Now on to our next trouble maker! Usually your Queens have BFFs called (in my parlance anyway) Wicked Poisoners. Poisoners are similar to Queens except they don't share the technical competencies that Queens have. What they excel at is stirring the pot so that no one notices their shortcomings.

I learned way too late in my management career that the most effective way to deal with Poisoners is to adopt the method that "what you start in public ends in public." Of course, conventional teaching says that employee issues should be dealt with in private. And for many situations that is absolutely true.

For too long, that is how I handled *all* employee situations, even the petty pot stirring ones. For example, if I was working with a person who was stirring up trouble, say, over a denied vacation request, I would bring the person into my office and explain why five people can't all be on vacation at the same time.

Of course, that person would then leave my office and go back to her group and complain, "It's not fair! It is the only week my husband can get off. She just doesn't like me!" The chances of her leaving my office and saying, "Wow, she has great reasons for why I can't take a vacation that week," are practically non-existent.

So I changed the method to my madness to what starts in public stays in public. And I gave my team fair warning. It wasn't long after that meeting that I was faced with my first opportunity to try out my new technique.

One day, someone came into my office and told me a nurse named Terri had spent most of the morning complaining about an ED nurse named Marcy's overtime. I knew I had my chance. In the past, I would have called Terri into my office and explained the overtime, but not today. I headed into the department and gathered everyone around the nurse's station.

"Come here for a second. This will only take a minute," I said. "Apparently, Terri has a problem with Marcy's overtime, and I thought maybe some of the rest of you might also."

They all looked down at the floor or out the window and muttered, "No, we're good. We don't have any problems."

"Okay," I continued, not believing this for a second. "Well, let me explain it to you anyway."

Basically, this was the deal: The hospital was opening an urgent care clinic, and HR decided that it would be more cost-effective to staff it with per diem nurses, who were at the time earning about $24.00 per hour, than it was to have the ED nurses work overtime, which would have come to about $27.00 per hour. But a proposal from Marcy to let her work overtime in the new clinic had been granted. Now, though Marcy had worked in the department for several years as a clerk and technician, she was a new RN. It seemed like she had been a nurse for a long time, when in reality she had just graduated and was earning new-grad pay.

So when she worked overtime her hourly salary was about $20.00 per hour, much less than the per diem nurses' amount. Marcy proposed that, because when she worked overtime her pay would be less than the per diem amount, she be allowed to pick up overtime hours. I presented her proposal to HR, and when I did, HR accepted.

I explained this to the staff (of course leaving out any specifics about salaries) and asked if they had any questions. Again, they all looked at the floor or out the window and said, "No, we're good. Thanks!"

When I walked back to my office, Terri was right on my heels. "I cannot believe you did that to me!" she huffed. "You violated my values!" She was even crying.

We stepped into my office and I asked her, "Did you come to me in private about Marcy's overtime or did you take it public? From now on, if you want things between the two of us to stay private, you need to make sure you don't take it public."

I went on to explain to her that I would be more than willing to discuss any issues she had in private and that she could come to me any time. My door would always be open. I also made it very clear that if she chose not to bring issues directly to me, and instead discussed matters with the entire team, then I would follow in the same direction and also discuss those issues with the entire team.

Now, I would love to be able to tell you that Terri changed her behavior and became a superstar, but it didn't happen. Terri didn't change, *but* her coworkers did. They knew that every time she started stirring the pot, I would come to them and give them an honest explanation of what was going on. I found that my team, like most other people, truly valued their leader's honesty. After a while Terri's credibility was diminished, and she didn't have an audience for her rants.

She still kept it up, and I had to let her know that her behaviors were not tolerable. I got HR involved early and eventually moved Terri out of our organization. And as leaders that's what you need to do: Just like with Queens, get HR involved early and take the necessary action to send those Poisoners packing.

If you are going to lead a successful team, you cannot do it with problem people on board. We've taken a close look at two common types, and sure, there are way more of them, but the way to deal with them is always the same.

They have to be stopped, and the very best way to stop them is to take away the power they possess over your team as a whole. Very often, that will mean getting them out of your organization.

It doesn't happen often, but once in a while a problem person will leave a team that no longer responds to the havoc they try to stir up. If a Queen doesn't have any "subjects," then she'll feel lost or out of place. The same applies to Poisoners. Without anyone to dispense their venom to, they cannot practice their craft and it makes them uncomfortable. And once these folks are off the team, it is so much easier to cultivate a constructive environment.

Obviously, you'll probably never be able to create the perfect team. There will always be people who are great when you hire them, but then don't live up to your expectations. Life happens. People change. As leaders, we have to be ready to either move or remove people from our organization when necessary. When you aren't afraid to tackle problem employees head-on, you can keep your positive employees happy and come as close to perfection as possible.

7

Surviving the Button Pushers: Calamity Janes, Red-Headed Stepchildren, and Red Meat Feeding Frenzies

No one ever said leading would be easy. (It's a good thing, huh?) And leading a team away from negativity is one of the toughest things you can do, *especially* if your culture has been negative for a long time.

Throughout this book, I give you strategies, tactics, and ideas for how to lead a positive, productive team. But make no mistake, I am not a Pollyanna. (You're probably thinking, *Gee, what was my first clue?*) I understand all too well how challenging it is to turn a culture around. And as I pointed out in the last chapter, there are certain people who seem to be deliberately bracing themselves against the other side of that 10,000-pound rock you're trying to push uphill.

Yes, there are people on your teams who will test you every opportunity they get. In this chapter, I want to share with you some skills everyone can use when they find leading these people taxing, trying, or tricky.

Once again, we'll do it by looking at those personalities who know exactly how to shake up your day. The difference is that the folks in this chapter aren't employees who need to be moved or removed. These are the people who push *our* buttons as leaders, but really aren't all that disruptive to the team. They might be annoying, but they aren't toxic.

The tips and advice I'll cover in this chapter will help you keep your button pushers in line so that you don't have to push them right out the door (or off a cliff!).

First up are the Calamity Janes. These folks create problems and then solve them. (Isn't that convenient?) Okay, maybe they don't create *all* the problems but they certainly have a sixth sense for hunting them down and an Olympic-athlete-level ability to make them much bigger than they really need to be.

Calamity Janes are self-appointed saviors. They like to feel like they're the only ones able to solve their department's, unit's, or company's problems.

That's how they gain their sense of self-worth. They like to feel indispensable.

Coming from healthcare, I've seen my fair share of Calamity Janes. I know they love to go to their leader and relay a story like, "Last night, when Joe was in charge we had something occur that could have been a disaster. But don't worry, *I* fixed it!" Then, they go on to sound like butter couldn't melt in their mouths, "Joe tries so hard when he is in charge, but he doesn't know the department like I do. I try to help out the best I can." Geez!

And I've seen nurses use the Calamity Jane approach a lot on unsuspecting leaders and coworkers. They point out what could have been a crisis, and then note exactly what they did to "fix" it. *Sure you fixed it,* I used to think, *you invented it!* Of course, the Calamity Janes I observed usually won because either their immediate leader or their coworkers would really start to think that this Calamity Jane or that Calamity Jane was the only one who could get things done.

So what do you do about them? Well, I'm sure there are various techniques that could work, but here's how I handled one of my biggest Calamity Janes:

When I was vice president of patient care, one of my night supervisors was a Calamity Jane. Every morning I would call in from my car on the way to work. (Don't worry, it was the early '90s so I wasn't on a cell phone. It was actually a hands-free mounted phone in the car. Very fancy!)

Each day it was the same. I would ask good ol' CJ how the night had gone and boy would she have an answer! She would, without fail, exclaim, "Oh MY, last night we had a BIG problem!"

"Really?" I would ask, inwardly cringing as I waited for the dramatic retelling. Then she would launch into a monologue about some tiny issue, usually something fairly routine, which in all reality probably took very little energy to solve. But this CJ would present it to me like she'd just gone through the nursing equivalent of Homer's *Odyssey*. I believe the other VP used to praise her for her daily reports, but not me!

Finally, I decided to put a stop to it. So one day, I sat her down and gave her a list of issues, which, were they to arise, I would consider to be "BIG problems." The list included things such as a baby is missing from the newborn nursery, a patient had been lost (and I don't mean as in deceased, I mean as in wandering the neighborhood!), or the hospital is on FIRE! I told Jane if the problem she experienced during the night shift was not on my list, it might well have been a problem, but it was not a BIG problem and she was banned from calling it such.

You're probably thinking, *Wow, Liz! That's harsh!* Maybe a little, but sometimes certain folks need to be reminded that we don't have BIG problems every day. We aren't slammed every day. And the place is not up for grabs every day. When you let Calamity Janes act like every day is the end times and they're the reason the organization survived, you are only promoting their disruptive behavior.

The good news is that I've found when you call a Calamity Jane on her craziness she'll usually make an effort to change her ways.

Next up, red-headed stepchildren. Now, I've mentioned red-headed stepchildren before so I think now is a good time to offer up a disclaimer. Some of you might *literally* have red-headed stepchildren, so please don't send me hate mail. I assure you I'm not talking about them. I'm talking about the figurative kind—specifically, those employees who paint themselves as the red-headed stepchildren of their unit, department, or company.

Usually, these are semi-low performers who excel at making you feel guilty about addressing their performance issues while taking very little responsibility for their own actions. When you call them in to talk, they highjack you. You might be in the middle of addressing an issue, and they'll say something like, "How would you know what goes on during the night shift? You are NEVER there. We NEVER see you! It's like we're the red-headed stepchildren of the department. Maybe if you were here more often, I would have more training and these mistakes wouldn't happen. It's really not my fault!"

And if you aren't prepared, you stumble right into their trap. You sit there open-mouthed. Your mind goes blank. It's like you momentarily forget the very valid point you were about to make, and somewhere in the back of your mind you start to think, *Well, she might be right. I'm not in the department as much as I would like to be.* (New leaders are especially susceptible to this trap.)

But know this: For these redheads you will never be there enough. If you're the executive director, it will be because you like other departments better. If you are the manager, it will be because you think your meetings are more important than your team members. And if you are a shift leader, it will be because you are in limbo between staff and leadership. Your red-headed stepchildren will tell you that you are becoming one of "them," meaning the higher-ups.

Your red-headed stepchildren want to drive you to give into what you perceive to be your own fears, inadequacies, and shortcomings so that you won't be nagging them about theirs.

Don't do it! Here's how to flip the switch on that whole conversation.

Let's say you are the shift leader and someone confronts you with, "You don't know what you're doing. You haven't been in this department long enough to know how things work. I can't even believe they put you in charge." You need to respond with a very calm, "It is true that I don't have as much experience as you, but I am committed to making tonight's shift great. I will not be able to do that without your cooperation. I hope you're on board."

That's it. That's all you need to say. Either they'll hop on board or they'll have to deal with the consequences of *not* being on board.

If you are a manager, you might hear, "I never get to see you. You are never here on my shift." The best way to quiet this is to say, "No, I'm not here every night that you work, but I am always available to you. You have my email, office phone number, and cell phone number. I make regular rounds on the night shift. However, if this is still inadequate for you and you really need to see more of me, the next time there is an opening on the day shift I will transfer you."

Now, this threat represents a worst nightmare scenario for an entrenched night shift nurse. You see, they usually love working when there aren't any suits around. However, sometimes they do put their red-headed stepchild wig on and use a leader's lack of presence on the nightshift against them. Whisper the words above, and they'll take that wig right off.

Executives probably won't hear this kind of complaint all that much, but every now and then a red-headed stepchild's gripe will make it all the way up the ladder. If you're a higher-up, there are some sure-fire ways to pacify those unruly redheads.

Ask your managers to bring you to the department (See Chapter 10 on managing up). When you do make these rounds, even if it is only a couple times a year, do something to make it memorable. Bring them doughnuts, popcorn, or some other treat. Invite team members from all your areas to a monthly or quarterly breakfast. This might not change the mind of your most stubborn guilt reapers, but it will change the mind of your team as a whole. And as we've touched on before, without a crowd to get behind them, your red-headed stepchildren won't have as much power.

My next "button pusher" isn't really a type of person so much as it's a situation that can pop up when your team is collectively having a bad day.

Sometimes we inadvertently teach our staff that they can get a big reaction from us if they demonstrate their own big reaction.

It's what Quint calls Red Meat Syndrome because it's like throwing red meat to a pack of wild, hungry dogs.

A problem percolates in the department. One person starts to talk about it, then another, and another. With each person, it becomes an even bigger problem. Eventually this "BIG" problem morphs into a juicy steak, and your staff is transformed into a pack of hungry dogs. They gnash their teeth at the problem. They wrestle it from one person to another. They begin to grumble and growl. BIG problem, BIG problem, we have a BIG problem!

You arrive on the scene and if you close your eyes, you can almost picture them tugging on the red meat like a pack of crazed canines. "What's wrong?" you exclaim. They immediately tell you, "WE HAVE A BIG PROBLEM!" And blam! Now the problem is all yours.

Your day changes instantly. Nope, I can't go to lunch; I've got a "BIG" problem. I'll have to miss that meeting. I have a "BIG" problem! Won't be home for dinner; I have a "BIG" problem!

Finally, you drag yourself away from work long after you normally would have left, but the "BIG" problem still looms. You think about it the entire drive home. You murmur a "Hello" to your family and advise them they're on their own tonight because you have a "BIG" problem. It even keeps you from sleeping. You toss…"BIG" problem…you turn…"BIG" problem.

Finally, the next day arrives and you drive to work and start in ready to face the "BIG" problem. You steady yourself and walk into the department ready to face the pack. And to your surprise, there are no hungry dogs. Nope, just gentle little lambs, every one. No "BIG" problems here! Wait, how can that be? I'll tell you my friends, THEY ATE IT!

Yep, the problem is gone. And it would have been gone in a matter of minutes yesterday, if you would have let it go. It's red meat so they would have gobbled it up. You realize you just wasted a ton of time on something that truly wasn't an issue.

This was the great lesson Quint taught me. You see, 99 percent of our big problems are *not* big problems; they are just red meat. As a leader, you need to be quick to assess issues and learn to recognize when you're just dealing with red meat.

Almost everything we face can wait 24 hours, and most problems will either disappear or work themselves out during that time.

And if the problem is still around after 24 hours, it's probably a legitimate issue. Address it calmly and reasonably. Then, move on.

So that's my two cents on the button pushers. You need to deal with Calamity Janes and red-headed stepchildren because they perpetually create problems. You probably don't have to worry too much about red meat feeding frenzies because they'll usually play themselves out.

Here's the good news: With the proper leadership, all of these people really are harmless. Just don't let them get under your skin. Trust me, Cupcakes, though it sounds easier than it actually is, eventually you *will* stop stressing over the button pushers. And when you reach that point (it took me years), you'll be a more effective leader and a much happier person.

8

Selection Savvy: Why You Should Forget about Attitude and Make Sure Your Recruits Can Follow Directions

Why is hiring so important in creating a positive work environment? To put it bluntly, it's because we practically NEVER fire anyone. At many organizations, once you're in, you're in for life—or until you leave on your own. But despite that fact, we don't always make the best hiring decisions.

Don't believe me? Just look over at Peter Passive Aggressive, who always says out loud, "Sure, no problem! Fantastic! I'll get right on it!" and then never makes another move. Or Ms. ADC (Avoiding Direct Confrontation), who will nod her head "yes" when her body language clearly screams, "NO!"

I know the so-called experts all say we should hire for attitude. That's easy when you have someone crazy enough to display a bad attitude right there in the interview. They're easy to weed out. The problem is that most people are smart enough to be at their very best during an interview. It's never, ever gonna get any better. And it usually gets a whole lot worse.

Here's my first piece of advice (and I know it sounds harsh): Don't give people you're interviewing the benefit of the doubt.

What you see is what you get. In other words, if the person is sloppily dressed, that's the best-case scenario for how he'll show up at work. If she gives one-word answers or seems bored, she's not going to be firecrackers once you hire her. And if he shows up late for the interview, (YEP, you guessed it!), he will be late for work on a regular basis. (If he had a wreck on his way in you might excuse him…but otherwise, forget it. He's wrong for you.)

So that's all well and good. And now I am going to let you in on a little secret: People in healthcare can be passive aggressive…GASP! I know, you're shocked. And I'm sure that's true in other industries, too. People in general are great at hiding their true (less than desirable) selves. It's pretty hard to hire for attitude when you are dealing with experts at passive-aggressive tendencies and other forms of attitude disguise.

Don't worry, though, I have a suggestion! Here's what I tell everyone who will listen to me (People listen to you, Liz? Ha! Yes, I have about two or three loyal followers): Hire people who follow your directions, listen to instructions, and do what is asked of them. Easy enough, right? I'll explain in a moment how to do this, but first let me give you an example that shows *why* following directions is so important.

Let's say you hire a great person with a perfect attitude. After she starts, you instruct her that every morning she needs to move the log book from the back counter to the front counter. She looks you right in the eye and exclaims, "No problem!" And you pat yourself on the back for making such a smart hire.

The next day you come to work and the log book is still on the back counter. So you gently remind her that it needs to be moved to the front counter. "You got it!" she cheers. And you think, *Well, that should do it. She'll take care of it now.*

But alas, on the third day the lonely log book remains on the back counter. So you give it one more try. You point to the log book, and she cries, "Oh, I am sorry! I forgot!"

Hmmm. Now you're really worried. On the fourth day, you decide to take matters into your own hands, literally, and physically take the log book from the back counter to the front. Your efforts are met with a very sweet smile. You tell yourself, *Surely this time she gets the picture…*but a nagging voice in the back of your mind suggests you might be deluding yourself.

On the fifth day, you can't even bear to look, so you wait until the next week. The next week Log Book Watch continues, and the news isn't any better. You approach the new hire and ask why she didn't move the log book. She looks at you as innocently as possible and says, "I thought you liked to be the one to move it. You did it last week." As our good friend Charlie Brown would say, "ARRRGGGGHHH!"

In between leadership jobs in nursing, I was a head hunter (Excuse me, I believe the PC term is professional recruiter), and one of the most valuable lessons I learned was to evaluate a person's ability to follow directions. What's the best way to do that? Give them an assignment.

Naturally, this is assuming you already know Hiring Rule #1, which is don't ever, ever, ever, EVER hire anyone after the first interview. *Always* have them come in for a second interview.

When you know this, you can give the potential hire an assignment during the first interview. I used to ask the person to come back with written answers to the following three questions:

1. What will you bring to this position?
2. What will you need from the organization in order to be successful?
3. What questions do you have about the position?

Make sure you are very clear that you want each question answered in writing. Ask them if they understand, and if they have any uncertainty about the assignment.

Pretty simple, right? Of course, you want to know their answers, but most importantly, you are assessing their ability to follow instructions. You won't believe how many people will show up for their second interview without having completed the assignment. But they *will* be ready with excuses, such as, "Oh, I didn't know you wanted it in writing. I am so sorry!" Well, they've made your job easier because now you can weed them out.

Others will have completed the assignment, but they'll hand it over to you messily scribbled on a napkin. They'll likely have an excuse of their own, explaining why they've just handed you a napkin. *Uh, how about you forgot about the assignment until you were out there in the waiting room, and a napkin is all you had to write anything on!*

Then there will be those beautiful souls who have it typed up, the questions bolded, the answers following with bullets. Perfect! They passed the first test.

But then you have to actually read what they wrote. In his answer to the question "What will you bring to this position?" one of my potential hires once wrote, "I am the smartest ED nurse out there, and I will be better than anyone you currently have on staff! I will teach all of them!" Alrighty, then...needless to say I didn't hire him. Fortunately, I really wasn't worried about destroying his self-esteem as he clearly had an abundance of self-confidence to fall back on.

There are other ways to test an individual's ability to follow directions. Tell them how to be successful at their next round of interviews. For example, while interviewing a potential hire you say, "Tell me about a time when you used humor to diffuse a difficult situation?" And his answer is perfect, humorous and brilliant. You know your team will love him and will appreciate his ability to think on his feet.

So you tell him that when he returns the next week, he'll be meeting with a group of his peers, and you believe they will love the story he just told. Instruct him to share it with the team when he meets with them. Remind him that even if that question is not asked, he should volunteer the story by saying, "When I met with Liz, she told me to share this story with you."

I mean, you can't make it any easier for a person than that! Now, you just have to sit back and see if he does it. If he fails to do so, don't hire him because he probably does not have what it takes to thrive in the organization. Not only did he not follow your instructions, but you also gave him insight into how to be successful with his potential peers, and he ignored it.

I emphasize following directions for two reasons. First off, the new hire is going to be the new guy or gal in the department, so when they start the job, it won't be surprising if they are good at following directions and learning. In fact, without my selection assignment, you might not figure out you've hired a Patty (or Peter) P.A. (Remember, that means passive aggressive. Not PIA, wink, wink, which is another type of problem altogether—look it up if you don't know what it means!) until long after the priceless and precious first 90 days.

Also it is a big indicator of whether or not she has what it takes to be successful at the organization. Does she have the ability to learn how to best work with the team? Can she get along with her peers? Is she willing to listen to others? And most importantly, does she listen to YOU?!? Much of this can be determined by giving potential newbies my "Follow These Instructions" assignment.

There are some very well-proven, successful tactics for evaluating a candidate's fit for the team, including prescreening candidates, peer interviewing, and behavioral-based interviewing. Try adding the tricks I just described to your process and you'll be one step closer to creating a team that makes being a leader one of the most gratifying jobs around.

It's simple. It's effective. It's cut and dried. You can make it a lot more complicated but why would you? Your life is hard enough already, right?

9

The Battle of We vs. They: Why No One Ever Wins

Bad news is hard to deliver. Sometimes, it's *very* hard to deliver. One reason is because we don't like letting people down. Another reason is we know people have a tendency to shoot the messenger—and hey, *we* certainly don't want to be shot. So we look around for a bulletproof vest, so to speak…and quite often that vest is in the closet labeled "W" for *We vs. They.*

Obviously, I fully understand how easy a trap *We vs. They* is to fall into. In fact, a little later in this chapter you'll see just how easy I know it is! Wanting to be liked (and not riddled with metaphorical bullets) is only human. But remember, we didn't sign up to be human; we signed up to be leaders. (Hmmm, that may have come out wrong.)

Anyway, as leaders, there will inevitably be situations when we have to tell our team members things that are tough and often things that we personally just don't like or agree with. When that happens, it is so much easier to shift the blame to someone else—like *your* boss—than to take the heat yourself.

We say things like, "If it were up to me, I would not have a problem with it, but you know Jenny, our VP, she won't budge an inch…" It's an easy habit to fall into because it takes you out of the hot seat and for that reason many leaders, at many levels, cave in to *We vs. They.* For example, you might then speak with Jenny, your VP, and hear her say, "I wouldn't even bring up this policy, but you know the suits at corporate are making me."

It goes on and on. The CEO blames the board. The board blames the community, and it never seems to end.

I was really good at playing this game. In fact, I got so good at it that I didn't even have to name names with my team. I had head nods and eye rolls to indicate which of the higher-ups was the bad guy on a given day. Mark Clement, our CEO, was a double head bob to the right. Quint, our COO at the time, was a double head bob to the left. And Brian, our CFO, was just a giant eye roll.

I would come back from meetings, and my team would ask, "Were you able to get the new equipment?" I would stand there looking defeated and use head bobs and high eye rolls to tell them which leader was being difficult. I wouldn't name names, but I would bob to the right and say, "He doesn't listen." Bob to the left, and say, "He doesn't care." Then, I'd finish with a giant eye roll and say, "And he is just impossible."

Of course, this was an excellent system because I came across as the good guy, and the administrative team was painted as wicked and evil. After awhile my team was convinced that I was the only leader in the entire organization who cared about them. Life was good for me.

Then one day, the entire organization did a 360 evaluation. You know the ones where your staff evaluates you, and they get to evaluate the administrative team as well. And if I remember correctly, they got to evaluate a bunch of other people. Basically, everyone gets to weigh in on everybody else.

The results came out, and I did very well. My team ranked me among the highest of all leaders if not *the* highest. As I read the rest of the report, I noticed my team did not give very high marks to the executive team. In fact, their scores were very, very low.

Shortly after the results came out, Mark called me into his office. I figured, *Man, these guys must really want to know how I do it.* And I was looking forward to giving them some advice.

The conversation started off pleasantly enough.

"So, Liz, your team gave you excellent evaluations," Mark C. began.

"Yes, I know," I replied, trying my best to sound humble while feigning concern—even though on the inside I was bursting with pride.

"They didn't rank the executive team so well," Mark C. continued.

They must really be taking this hard, I thought to myself. "Yes, I saw that," I said, infusing concern into my voice as I tried to repress a smirk.

"And where, exactly, do you think your team gets their opinions about the executive team?"

Uh oh.

I started to look around the room, out the window, at my shoes, anywhere but at him. Finally, I had to speak.

"Hmmm, I dunno, me?"

"Exactly!" he replied. "And I am putting you on notice right now that the next time we have an evaluation, your scores and ours will be much better matched or else your future as a leader in this organization will be in jeopardy. Am I clear?"

Oh, he was! Crystal clear, and boy, was I mad! I thought, *On what planet is it my job to make these guys look good?!?* So I did what I always do when I am in a jam: I called my friend Mark Albarian. (If you read *Eat That Cookie!*, you know that he is the guy I always bug for advice. Then when he gives it to me I spend an hour telling him why he is wrong. And then, of course, the next day I realize he is a genius…now if you didn't read the first book, I've just told you why Mark Albarian is a close, dear friend.)

So I pull him out of a meeting somewhere in LA, and I start whining and complaining, "I can't believe this administration of mine! They expect me to make them look good in the eyes of my staff."

So my dear friend started asking me questions.

"Well, Liz, does the staff interact that much with the executive team?"

"No," I answered.

"How do they know them?" he asked.

"Um, basically from me," I admitted.

Then he paused and said, "Okay, then let me ask you one more tough one. Does it help the ED staff to think that the people you report to are idiots, meanies, or jerks?"

I took a moment, because I knew he had me cornered. Finally, I relented, "No, it doesn't help the staff to think that the administrative team are goofs." I felt like I was admitting that I took the last cookie out of the jar or the last cupcake in the break room.

"Well then, Liz, that is why you have to make 'those guys' look good. Not for the executives in general, but for your team."

I didn't even have to wait a day on that one. I knew my friend was right.

It did not help the team to think that the higher-ups were cold, uncaring, or worse yet, incompetent. And as a leader, I had to grow up and realize I could no longer make them the bad guys for every tough thing that came up.

So, my dear Cupcakes, let's stop saying things like, "Let me run that by Jenny," or, "I will ask Bob the next time I see him."

If a team member asks something like, "Why can't we get new computers?" don't say, "I would love to! Unfortunately, I'll have to ask Jenny, and she'll probably say no." If you know the answer is no, then just say so with an explanation.

Something like this might work: "It would be great to get new computers. Lord knows we need them! But this is a tough budget year and every department is being asked to keep costs down. Now is just not the right time for us to spend the money on new computers."

Some of you might be wondering, *What should I do when I really don't know the answer?* Then, instead of putting the burden on Jenny or Bob, say something like, "Let me research that." Or say, "I will look into that and get back to you."

Of course, you can still ask Jenny, but when she says no don't take it back to the team as "Jenny's decision." Instead, go back and say something like: "I have looked into getting new computers for the department and have found that now is not a good time, because this is a tough budget year and blah, blah, blah."

Take ownership of the tough decisions. It is truly better for your team.

They are adults. They can take the truth. Unlike Tom Cruise in *A Few Good Men*, they CAN handle the truth. And when you take ownership of the bad news as well as the good news, your team will see you as a stronger leader. Not someone who is always rejected by administration, not someone who can't get things done, but as a leader who understands both the department's and the organization's needs.

I learned a lot about eliminating *We vs. They* from Quint. If you have read his books or have heard him speak, you know that he believes this is one of the most dangerous mistakes leaders make. It weakens an organization because it undermines its leadership team and upsets the staff. And really that is minor when compared to what *We vs. They* does to you all as leaders. So please don't do it. Don't get sucked into it.

Instead, do something so much more productive...something so much more beneficial for you and your team. What is it?!? Turn the page, Cupcakes, and you'll learn all about it in the next chapter.

10

Manage Up Your Boss: Why a Little Butt-Kissing with a Purpose Can Do Great Things for You and Your Team

If you're familiar with Quint's philosophy, you probably know about managing up. He teaches leaders how to position people at all levels of an organization in a positive light in order to improve performance, unify corporate culture, and generally spread goodwill. These are all great benefits, of course, and I highly recommend managing up for all of these reasons.

In this chapter, though, I want to be a little less PC about it. I want to discuss managing up in its purest form—using it to finagle interactions with higher-ups. Yep, that's right: Managing up can make life a lot easier for you and your team.

No, I am not talking about sucking up to the boss for self-serving reasons, nor am I talking about butt-kissing just for the sport of it.

I'm talking about the art form that is managing up the boss. (Okay, I'll admit you might consider this a form of butt-kissing...but it's butt-kissing with a higher purpose.) When you do it right, *everyone* wins.

Like most things in my life, I learned about managing up the hard way. As you know, my experience with the 360 evals did not turn out well for me. I had to change the way I represented the leadership of the organization to my staff. I also had to work on building favorable relationships between me, my staff, and senior leaders.

I knew I had to do these things, but honestly, I had no idea how to get started. Then one day I listened to Quint explain the techniques of managing up. I learned four major lessons from that chat about managing up your boss and your boss's boss:

- Represent relief, not grief.
- Remember your boss is human.
- Keep the boss in your pocket.
- Go for the triple win.

Let's take a detailed look at each of them.

Represent relief, not grief.

In every interaction with your boss, you should represent relief. In other words, the boss should always be happy to see you. I hear all of the time from people who tell me that it seems as though their boss ignores them. If you think that's true, then you need to ask yourself, *Am I a Debbie Downer or a Bummer Bob when I am in their office? Do I speak to him or her only when I'm facing a problem, an unpleasant issue, or need a boost?*

Don't get me wrong. Most bosses are pretty good at helping with all of that, but who would want to do it all the time?

In order to make this easier to understand, think about how you'd feel if the people on your team used you in the same way. Imagine anyone on your team saying to you, "Hey, do you have a second? I need to talk to you." Okay, now separate your entire team into two groups:

> Group Relief: the employees who wouldn't strike instant fear in your heart the minute they approached you—in fact, they might bring a sense of relief.

and…

> Group Grief: the ones who scare you to death with those words because you know they're about to lead you into a world of pain.

Now, let's say both groups have the same issue. They want to tell you that someone called in sick for the night shift. Members of Group Grief are most likely to emit a heavy sigh, shake their head, and say something like, "I hate to tell you this, but Terry called in sick for the night shift tonight. It's going to be really bad, because they were already short one person, and we have been too busy to call to see if anyone else could work!" *Waa, Waa...Gripe, Gripe...Complain, Complain...etcetera.*

And now, here's the same scenario with Group Relief: "Hey, I wanted to tell you that Terry called in sick for tonight, and as they were already down one person, I knew it would make things tough. So I called Pat, and she is able to come in tonight if we give her Friday off. Since this is only Monday, it gives us four days to fix Friday and solves the immediate crisis." *Ahhh, relief!*

So those are the people who work for you. Now think about the way you approach your boss. Which group would he or she put you in? Quint tells the funniest story about when he was CEO and someone sent him an email with the subject line, "HEADS UP...All the surgeons upset today in the OR. You might want to stop in down there." He ends the story with an adamant, "I don't think so!"

His point, of course, was that whoever composed that email sent a lot of grief when they hit "send." Who in their right mind would want to go down into an OR full of unhappy surgeons? Instead, that person might have offered him some possible solutions on what might turn those surgeons' frowns upside down!

That's managing up. The idea is to make the boss WANT to hear from you so that he or she will WANT to be cooperative and make your job easier.

Remember your boss is human.

I know! It's hard to believe, but it is true. That means that every boss has strengths and weaknesses that we should take into consideration. It is not a hard thing to do if you are willing to take the time to figure out what your boss excels at and in what areas you might be able to lend a helping hand.

For example, as a leader I was never all that good with financials. At one point, the hospital where I was working was thinking of starting up an off-site clinic, and one of my managers was working on a feasibility and implementation study. She put the whole thing together, and then it just sat on my desk for longer than I'd like to admit. I know it was frustrating to her, but the thought of verifying and crunching all those numbers just made me put it off day after day.

Now had that manager known that finance was a weakness of mine, she could have worked things out a little better for both of us. For example, it would have been great if before she put the study on my desk she had run the numbers by our CFO. Then she could have attached a note reading, "Hi Liz, Here is the off-site study. I already ran the numbers past Brian, and he says they look good!"

Wow! Wouldn't that have been easier for both of us? I could have then quickly looked at the operational issues, knowing that the financials were fine, and poof! We would have been off and running and she wouldn't have had to wait and wait for my feedback.

In contrast, we can also use our boss's strengths to work better and smarter. Clearly, one of Quint's strengths is in developing individual talent. So if I was ever struggling with a team member who was a middle performer, but who I knew had the potential and willingness to move up to a high performer, I would often ask him for his insight. It usually never took that long, maybe 30 minutes maximum, but I was always grateful for his expertise.

I also think because this was an area he truly enjoyed, he was more than happy to share the time with me. By acknowledging his strength in this area, I made him feel good, and, as a bonus, it made my job easier too.

Keep your boss in your pocket.

Okay, now don't go calling Human Resources on me. Of course, I don't literally mean keep your boss in your pocket (as in, he's a tiny mouse) or figuratively (as in, you're buying his influence). Either option could certainly make things awkward!

It's really more about pretending your boss is with you all the time—like, maybe on speaker phone in your pocket.

Think about how differently your day would go. It would certainly eliminate a lot of the we/they stuff that comes so naturally for some of us. It also would help us remember to walk the walk. That is a hard thing to do. Indeed, sometimes it is even hard to do when your boss is with you in person.

At Holy Cross, one of our standards required us to pick up trash when we came upon it. One day I was walking with Quint from a building across the street from the main hospital. We passed an object at the curb next to the sidewalk. He looked at me and asked, "Aren't you going to pick that up?"

"No," I responded, knowing that a sermon would follow and it did. "You know, Liz, as a leader you have to set an example. Even though you are not in your department right this minute, there could still be employees watching you. Someone might be looking out one of the hospital windows or driving past us. As a leader you have to follow the standards; otherwise you can't really expect anyone else to. Now, don't you think you should pick that up?"

"But Quint," I protested, "it's a hubcap!"

Okay, so maybe he was being JUST A BIT over the top with his insistence that I pick up a 10-pound, grease-covered hunk of metal, but his point was well taken. It's usually a good idea to act as if all eyes are trained on you at all times.

In addition to helping you walk the walk, keeping your boss with you at all times helps you to manage up your boss when he or she isn't there.

This benefits you as much as it does your boss. You can do this both with your team and with your boss's boss.

For example, one time, I was conducting a committee meeting that Mark C. was supposed to attend. Unfortunately, he was called away to something more urgent. He asked me to stop by, and as he was explaining why he couldn't attend, he handed me an article. He said he was going to hand it out to the team because he thought the author had made some really good points pertinent to the work the committee was doing. He asked me to make sure everyone got a copy.

Now I could have just gone to the meeting, explained that Mark got called away, conducted our business, and then at the end passed out copies of the article. Instead, I figured out that it would be better for the team, Mark, and me if I said, "Mark is sorry that he can't be with us today, but he wanted to share this article with all of you. He said when he came across it he thought about the great work our committee was doing."

See? Not hard, but a totally different, positive twist. Positioning Mark in that way was a great, easy way for me to manage him up in the eyes of his employees, which will probably be reflected the next time they do 360 evaluations. I made it so it was as if Mark was right there with us...and I guess he kinda was...in my pocket!

Go for the triple win.

Love, love, LOVE the triple win. I learned this over the years too. If it is important for your team to have a senior leader present for a major event, make sure he or she is there. Then go beyond that and make sure the superstars on your team get recognized and that the event is a success…that, my dear Cupcakes, is the essence of the triple win. (You'll see what makes it "triple" momentarily.)

Let me set the scene. Cathy is the manager of Outpatient Imaging. In the past quarter, their patient satisfaction scores rose from the 40th percentile to the 75th. I am the vice president Cathy reports to. Cathy decides to have cake one afternoon to celebrate the team's accomplishment. She thinks that it would mean a lot to the team if a senior leader was present. So instead of picking a date and just *hoping* that I can be there, she calls my office and finds out what afternoon I have open to spend a half hour with her team.

As I approach the department on the day of the celebration, Cathy takes no chances that I might screw things up. She meets me and fills me in on everything she thinks I need to know.

"Hi, Liz, as you might remember this team has gone from the 40th percentile to the 75th in just one quarter. They have all worked very hard, and I am just so proud of them. I am really proud of the work that Bob did on our communication bulletin board. That board served as a centerpiece for the initiative and he did a great job. Oh, and one more thing before you go in. Remember, Linda is on her final disciplinary action before being terminated."

Now with this last point you might be thinking, *Wow, Cathy! Way to bring down the mood!* But here is why that is so perfect: It keeps me from walking in and saying to Linda, "Great job. So glad you are part of the team." (Could be beyond awkward, right?)

The reason for the rest of the information is more obvious. It keeps me from making a mistake about the scores. And it tells me I should give Bob a special shout-out. More importantly, though, Cathy has given me the information I need to make her entire team feel really proud about everything they've accomplished.

As the cake is cut, I address the group. "I am so happy to be here with you today to celebrate your great accomplishment in patient satisfaction. Going from the 40th to the 75th is amazing, and Cathy has been bragging about your hard work to the entire leadership team. She is so proud of all of you. Bob, Cathy told me that your work on that communication board was pivotal to the team's success. She said it really brought the group together, and you worked diligently to make sure it stayed updated and fresh. Thanks so much for such an important contribution. "

Then I go on to say a few more words, and then it is cake time...or should I say cupcake time!

Now, as promised, here is why this little strategy is called the triple win:

1. *Winner #1: Bob and the Team*—First of all, the whole team feels good about their accomplishment. Bob, in particular, is glowing with pride. How do you think he is feeling about me right now? Pretty good, don't you think? And I'll bet all of them are thinking the world of Cathy. I mean how nice to have a boss who says such great things to the executive!

2. *Winner #2: Cathy*—I'll bet she is very proud of her team right now, and happy that she could get them all (especially Bob) some much-deserved recognition. As I mentioned, she's feeling the love from them, too. Hopefully, she is also thinking that I am a pretty cool boss.

3. *Winner #3: Me*—I am so happy to share a good time with this team. It's certainly the highlight of my day, and I am glad that I found out about the special work that Bob has done. I also think because I said good things about Cathy when I was speaking—namely that she had been bragging to the executives—that it made me more credible as a complimenter and probably made Cathy proud as well. And I am thinking I must have been a genius when I hired her. After all, look at all she did to make me look great today.

And that, my fellow Cupcakes, is the snazzy little technique I learned called the triple win. Try it! You will be surprised how much it helps to build pride and get you points with the boss, both of which are pretty good things.

Managing up your boss doesn't just make things better for you (that would be self-serving) or better for the big kahuna (even if it does sometimes feel a little like butt-kissing). Most importantly, it makes things better for your team. The interactions we have with our bosses most definitely affect all of those people with whom we work. As we improve the relationships with our bosses, we improve the workplace for all.

11

Just *Tell Them* Already! (Stop Being a Namby-Pamby and SPEAK UP to Get What You Need)

The Rolling Stones let us all know that while you can't always get what you want, when you try sometimes, you just might find, you get what you need. Notice the Stones DIDN'T say, "…when you sit around hoping, people will intuitively know what you need and give it to you." No, they said WHEN YOU TRY, you get what you need. Well, Cupcakes, TRYING isn't that hard. It just means not being a namby-pamby. It means telling people what you need.

Of course, as with all things leadership, that's easier said than done. I find that it's especially difficult for those leaders who were born with, or have developed over time, a keen, sharpened ability to know what other people need. If you're one of these sensitive souls, you can sense what your patients, students, customers, or colleagues need simply by reading a gesture or listening between the lines. Sometimes you know what these folks need before they even realize they need it.

The downside of such a skill is that because you're so good at understanding what others need you naturally assume everyone else does, too. And you just as naturally assume that the people around you—your coworkers, bosses, even family members—should be able to know what *you* need, too.

Unfortunately, usually they *don't* know. They really truly haven't the slightest idea. And that can lead to all kinds of ugly complications and hurt feelings.

Often, when people fail to help or soothe you, you assume it is because they don't care or that they're simply unwilling to lend a helping hand. But that is not the case. It is simply because they really don't know, and they need you to tell them.

If you would only *tell* people (nicely, of course!) what you need, they would be most happy to give it...so darn it, why won't you just do it?

I think this kind of misunderstanding happens in relationships all the time. It has certainly happened to my husband, Frank, and me. We just celebrated our 30th anniversary. And over the years, I would like to think that I have gotten better at telling him what I need. However, when we were newlyweds, that was not always the case.

Shortly after we were married, my sister moved to New Jersey. The whole family went out to visit her for Christmas. My parents, Frank, and I all flew together, and the visit lasted for about a week. My niece and nephew were very young, and it was fun to be around little ones for Santa's big night.

In fact, waiting for Santa with the kids is the only viable explanation I can give for the hideous nightgown I wore on that trip. It was red flannel with big white ruffles around the collar and cuffs. Now, if you have ever seen me, I am a very big woman, so suffice it to say there was A LOT of red flannel. I was called "Mrs. Claus" by my sister Donna on more than one occasion on that visit. The photographs from Christmas morning still give me the shivers!

Other than that red flannel nightgown the trip went well until the night before we were coming home when I got a terrible stomach flu. It was a rough night, and I probably should not have flown the next day, but I was determined to get home. We did make our flight, but it was not pleasant as I was throwing up the whole time.

We finally landed and got to our car. I was happy to be back in Chicago, but still feeling pretty terrible. We had almost made it all the way to our house when I felt another horrible wave of nausea. Frank pulled over in a vacant parking lot, and I leapt out of the car and was sick again.

Now, here I am standing almost doubled over in an empty lot, feeling terrible and no doubt looking even worse. My parents are peering out from the back seat, and I don't want to get back in the car all a mess. I desperately need something to wipe my face with but of course there is nothing in sight. Not a towel or even a rag. Then, I thought of that silly red nightgown. In my mind it was perfect for the job because I didn't care if I ever wore that thing again. I thought, *I can use it and leave it in the trash right here in the parking lot. Then, I never have to see it again.*

I shouted to Frank, "Honey, will you get me that red nightgown from my suitcase?"

I was still kind of bent over at this point, but when he came over, I could see him out of the corner of my eye, standing next to me, holding the nightgown by both arms fully extended and sort of "presenting" it to me. As if I was going to put the thing on right there next to the street for all of Chicago to see!

"Give it to me," I hissed, trying to yank the flannel monstrosity out of his hands.

"Let me help you," he insisted, trying to get it over my head.

"I am NOT going to put it on!" I yelled.

"Then why did you have me get it out of the suitcase?" he demanded.

"So I could wipe my face, you fool," I snapped at him.

"Then you should have said so…I keep a towel in the trunk," he said.

"A towel!" (*would have been so much better*) I exclaimed. "Well, if you REALLY LOVED ME, you should have known what I needed!"

"Are you kidding me? Do you come with a manual? Because I need to read the page about a red nightgown in a parking lot!" he hissed.

Oh, we must have been quite the sight! A car brimming with awkward post-holiday togetherness idling in an empty parking lot next to a highway whizzing with traffic…my new husband forcing a huge red nightgown over my head, while we yelled at each other…my poor parents trying hard not to stare at the train wreck that was the two of us. (Good times!)

The point is I thought for sure Frank would know that I just needed something for my face. How could he *not* know that?!? But clearly he did not, AND I had failed to tell him what I really needed. I'm sure that wiping my face was the last thing that Frank would have thought of when I asked for the nightgown. Back then, when we were newlyweds, I thought that because we loved each other it meant that we would always know what the other person needed…WRONG!

To really believe this is the height of naivety. (Even those who are very good at sensing the needs of others guess wrong sometimes!) And if you think about it, it's also the height of self-centeredness. Why would you assume everyone in the world thinks like you do? (Weren't you supposed to outgrow that belief in childhood?)

All of this applies in the workplace, too. Somehow, too many of us think our bosses should automatically know what we need from them at any given moment. How could they not? I mean, if they're a good boss they should just "get it," shouldn't they?

As someone with a lot of experience as a leader, allow me to let you in on a secret—we are not clairvoyant. And you probably wouldn't want us to be. ("Here, Gertrude, let me give you that new computer program you've been needing...and by the way, congrats on beating your high score at Angry Birds while you were supposed to be working!")

For another, I think we often hold our bosses under a microscope that most of us would not want to be under ourselves.

If your boss is expected to know what you need, then shouldn't *you* know what *she* needs before she ever gives you the assignment? (See how silly that sounds?)

When I was the CNO at Holy Cross Hospital, there was an opening for the manager position of the Telemetry Unit. I filled the position with a nurse named Linda. She had been a nurse on the night shift for many years, but this was to be her first management position.

About six months after she had accepted her new role, I held a mini town hall meeting in the lounge of the Telemetry Unit. Linda was not there. This meeting was an opportunity for me to get a feel for what was on her staff members' minds.

The group was quiet so I started by asking some direct questions. First I asked, "So how is Linda doing in her new position?"

The group responded quickly, "Good! You can really tell she is trying very hard. The schedule isn't perfect, but Linda gets it out soon enough so we have time to fill in the holes before there are any staffing disasters. We also finally got those IV pumps we have been waiting for..."

"Great! Glad to hear it," I responded. Then I probed a little further. "Is there anything that Linda could improve upon?"

They hesitated just a moment before saying, "Well, Linda doesn't really compliment us much. We work really hard here on this unit, and it would be nice, just once in awhile, to hear her say, 'Good job,' or, 'Nicely done.'"

"Oh, I agree," I said. "I think it is very important. I will have a discussion with Linda about recognition."

The group seemed worried. One member said, "We don't want to get Linda in trouble. We know she has been working very hard. She gets here by 6:30 every morning and often is still here at 7 p.m. when the night shift arrives. It's just nice to hear a compliment now and then."

"I understand," I said. Then I asked the group, "So, how many of you have complimented Linda in the last six months?"

They looked stunned. Then, they looked at each other and shrugged their shoulders.

"Why do you ask that?" one of them questioned.

"Well, you all just told me that when you are working really hard it is nice to receive a compliment," I said. "You also told me that Linda has been working really hard. So, it would seem to me that one or more of you would have let her know that you've noticed and appreciated her efforts."

Now, how many of Linda's staff do you think would have had to compliment her before Linda figured out that she should be recognizing her team? If you said one...DING, DING, DING...you are correct!

Another thing to keep in mind is that the little things your leaders do that upset you probably fly under their radar. I once had a night supervisor named Barb. I resented her just because when she made rounds she would say, "Keep it quiet, girls." OHHH, I couldn't stand that! It was condescending, demeaning, and just plain wrong. Keep it quiet, my eye! Like we wanted it to be busy! Like we had any control over it! Man, it bugged me!

Looking back, I'm guessing that I was the person at fault in that situation. I doubt that Barb expected us to keep it quiet. She was most likely just wishing us a quiet shift. I am sure her intentions were good. And if it bothered me so much, I should have told her. I'll bet she would have changed her watchwords to "Have a good shift" or something similar.

Barb wasn't a bad supervisor. I had simply failed to tell her what I needed. And when I think about how much time I wasted being resentful, it just makes me shake my head.

To sum it all up, there are many ways of telling people what you need. In Frank's case, I should have been more explicit in my request. In Linda's situation, her team could have role modeled the way they needed to be recognized. And with Barb, I could have let her know why her phrase bothered me.

Don't be afraid to tell people what you need! And make sure your team knows it's A-OK to ask you for what they need. It makes for a much more pleasant workplace because it eliminates the potential for toxic resentment to build up over time. You'll get what you need as a leader, and you'll be able to give your team what they need right back.

Conclusion

Hey, Cupcakes!
Never Be Afraid to
Laugh at Your Mistakes

Leaders are ordinary people doing extraordinary things.

I say this every time that I speak on leadership. I said it in the introduction of this book. And now, I'm ending it with this thought.

You all need to realize the work you do is extraordinary. Stop worrying about what you don't know. Stop worrying about making mistakes. Stop worrying about letting others down. The fact that you step up and try while others sit back means you are a leader. You help your teams discover their talents. You bring hope to the workplace. And most importantly, you inspire people to do their best.

That said, don't ever forget to have fun. In *Eat That Cookie!*, I devoted an entire chapter to fun and how essential it is for creating a positive workplace. As leaders, we're sometimes called to do very serious work, to take on very serious responsibilities, but darn it, sometimes we just need to lighten up and stop taking OURSELVES so seriously!

I like to think that I have a master's degree in lightening up. As many of the stories I've shared throughout the book have indicated, Cupcakes, I've made a lot of (often hilarious) mistakes. (Remember my CABG story? Neither I nor that nurse thought that was very funny in the moment, but I can't help but chuckle when I look back on it. If, at the time, the nurse and I had just laughed at my mistake or if she had, at the very least, just patted me on my goofy little head, we would both have had a much brighter day.)

Sometimes the only way to deal with your mistakes is to laugh them off! Honestly, I can't even count the ways I have screwed up as a leader, from simple things like forgetting to order supplies to hugely embarrassing things like falling out of my chair at a department head meeting (Yes, that really happened! They don't call me Grace for no reason.) to major snafus like forgetting to budget for vacation time or hiring the worst person in the world.

It happens to all of us. Well, hopefully you won't all start falling out of your chairs, but you get what I'm saying! It is okay to admit to making a mistake, and when you can infuse a good dose of humor into the situation, it's even better.

To really drive that point home, I am going to share a final story about one of my biggest leadership blunders. It was a classic Liz moment, and because I have such a warped sense of humor, it still makes me laugh today.

When I was a young nurse leader at Christ Hospital, I was part of the Critical Care Division. It was a large division comprised of eight ICUs and the ED. The Critical Care Division also had some clinical specialists who were a part of the leadership team, so in all, when we met as a team, there were about 12 of us.

We reported to a division leader who was ambitious, brilliant, and very driven to move up in the organization. She really wasn't that much older than most of us. In fact, at the time, she was still in her late 20s, but because she was so serious, she always seemed sooo much older to us. Though to be fair, I'm sure to her we all seemed like a bunch of goofballs! (Correction, we *were* a bunch of goofballs, as you're about to see.)

So one day we were gathered in a meeting room just off the hospital cafeteria for a division leadership meeting. Our oh-so-serious division leader was running late, which wasn't like her at all. While the rest of us were waiting, I spotted a big box of those really tall white chef hats in the corner of the room.

Now, I am somewhat of a fatalist so I believed that if the universe places a box of chef hats in your meeting room, you are meant to wear them. As the Leader of the Goofballs, I started passing them out. We all put them on, laughing and giggling like a bunch of teenage girls at a slumber party. I told you we were goofballs!

We heard our leader coming so we quieted down and folded our hands on the table trying to look as serious as we could with really tall chef hats on. The door opened, and in walked the corporate head of human resources (Yep, "corporate," as in not just head of the hospital, but the entire organization!) Behind him was our leader.

She looked appalled and aghast. Judging by the look she was giving us, you'd think we were all sitting around that conference table naked. To her credit, though, she didn't say much. She just calmly took her seat next to the HR executive and ushered a quiet command, "Take off the hats." Then, she proceeded with the business at hand.

Can you imagine what a disaster that was? I'm sure she was mortified. And we goofballs had just broken several key rules right in front of a corporate big shot, including misappropriation of hospital supplies and inappropriate behavior for a leader. We were *so* far from perfect that day, but you know what, we WERE having fun!

I could probably fill a book with all the ways that I have messed up in my leadership career. (Wait, I think I just did!) But I've never let them get in the way of my love for being a leader. In fact, if anything, I think my mistakes and my ability to laugh at them has made being a leader even more fulfilling.

I hope you won't let your mistakes get in the way of becoming a wonderful leader. I know how easy it can be to get disheartened or lost along the way. That is why, my dear Cupcakes, I have written this book to give you a boost when you need it. Pick it up when you need some guidance or when you just need to laugh at the crazy lady who falls out of chairs and wears chef hats during important meetings.

With *Hey Cupcake!*, I so much wanted to share the secrets that I have learned along the way—things I wish someone had told me early on in my career, things that would have kept me from becoming discouraged. I hope something I've said in this book resonated with you in a way that you can use in your own leadership journey.

It all comes down to this: The most important thing you can do is be true to yourself. When you believe that you are doing the right thing for the right reason, you will be a great leader. Don't let the mistakes you make along the way ever get in the way of that. And don't ever let your pursuit of being a great leader get in the way of having a little fun!

"A deeply held belief in doing what's right is what energizes a leader to lead and inspires others to follow no matter what obstacles they may encounter."

—BG Porter, CEO, Studer Group

Resources to Help
You Thrive in the
Pay-for-Performance Era

Access additional resources at www.studergroup.com.

ABOUT STUDER GROUP:

Studer Group® helps bring structure and focus to organizations through the creation of cultures of accountability. We have partnered with over 850 healthcare organizations in the U.S. and beyond to achieve and sustain exceptional clinical, operational, and financial outcomes. As they face ever-greater quality demands—HCAHPS, Core Measures, preventable readmissions, hospital-acquired conditions, and more—they engage us to help them create cultures of execution. Using our Evidence-Based Leadership^{SM} framework as the starting point, we hardwire processes that get them aligned, accountable, and agile so they can execute proven tactics quickly, consistently, and in the right sequence...and sustain the results over time. We also help them foster better integration with physicians and other service providers in order to create a smooth continuum of patient-centered care.

STUDER GROUP COACHING:

Healthcare Organization Coaching

As value-based purchasing changes the healthcare landscape forever, organizations need to execute quickly and consistently, achieve better outcomes across the board, and sustain improvements year after year. Studer Group's team of performance experts has hands-on experience in all aspects of achieving breakthrough results. They provide the strategic thinking, the Evidence-Based Leadership framework, the practical tactics, and the ongoing support to help our partners excel in this high-pressure environment. Our performance experts work with a variety of organizations, from academic medical centers to large healthcare systems to small rural hospitals.

Emergency Department Coaching

With public reporting of data, healthcare organizations can no longer accept crowded Emergency Departments and long patient wait times. Our team of ED coach experts will partner with you to implement best practices, proven tools, and tactics using our Evidence-Based Leadership approach to improve results in the Emergency Department that stretch or impact across the entire organization. Key deliverables include improving flow, decreasing staff turnover, increasing employee, physician, and patient satisfaction, decreasing door-to-doctor times, reducing left without being seen rates, increasing upfront cash collections, and increasing patient volumes and revenue.

Physician Integration & Partnership Coaching

Physician integration is critical to an organization's ability to run smoothly and efficiently today and to do more with less in a financially challenging future. Studer Group coaches diagnose how aligned physicians are with your mission and goals, train you on how to effectively provide performance feedback, and help physicians develop the skills they need to prevent burnout. The goal is to help physicians become engaged, enthusiastic partners in the truest sense of the word—which optimizes HCAHPS results and creates a better continuum of high-quality patient care.

To learn more about Studer Group coaching, visit www.studergroup.com.

BOOKS: categorized by audience

Senior Leaders & Physicians

Leadership and Medicine—A book that makes sense of the complex challenges of healthcare and offers a wealth of practical advice to future generations, written by Floyd D. Loop, MD, former chief executive of the Cleveland Clinic (1989-2004).

Engaging Physicians: A Manual to Physician Partnership—A tactical and passionate roadmap for physician collaboration to generate organizational high performance, written by Stephen C. Beeson, MD.

Straight A Leadership: Alignment, Action, Accountability—A guide that will help you identify gaps in Alignment, Action, and Accountability, create a plan to fill them, and become a more resourceful, agile, high-performing organization, written by Quint Studer.

Excellence with an Edge: Practicing Medicine in a Competitive Environment—An insightful book that provides practical tools and techniques you need to know to have a solid grasp of the business side of making a living in healthcare, written by Michael T. Harris, MD.

Physicians

Practicing Excellence: A Physician's Manual to Exceptional Health Care—This book, written by Stephen C. Beeson, MD, is a brilliant guide to implementing physician leadership and behaviors that will create a high-performance workplace.

All Leaders

The Great Employee Handbook: Making Work and Life Better—This book is a valuable resource for employees at all levels who want to learn how to handle tough workplace situations—skills that normally come only from a lifetime of experience. *Wall Street Journal* bestselling author Quint Studer has pulled together the best insights gained from working with thousands of employees during his career.

The HCAHPS Handbook: Hardwire Your Hospital for Pay-for-Performance Success—A practical resource filled with actionable tips proven to help hospitals improve patient perception of care. Written by Quint Studer, Brian C. Robinson, and Karen Cook, RN.

Hardwiring Excellence—A *BusinessWeek* bestseller, this book is a road map to creating and sustaining a "Culture of Service and Operational Excellence" that drives bottom-line results. Written by Quint Studer.

Results That Last—A *Wall Street Journal* bestseller by Quint Studer that teaches leaders in every industry how to apply his tactics and strategies to their own organizations to build a corporate culture that consistently reaches and exceeds its goals.

Hardwiring Flow: Systems and Processes for Seamless Patient Care—Drs. Thom Mayer and Kirk Jensen delve into one of the most critical issues facing healthcare leaders today: patient flow.

Eat That Cookie!: Make Workplace Positivity Pay Off...For Individuals, Teams, and Organizations—Written by Liz Jazwiec, RN, this book is funny, inspiring, relatable, and is packed with realistic, down-to-earth tactics to infuse positivity into your culture.

"I'm Sorry to Hear That..." Real-Life Responses to Patients' 101 Most Common Complaints About Health Care—When you respond to a patient's complaint, you are responding to the patient's sense of helplessness and anxiety. The service recovery scripts offered in this book can help you recover a patient's

confidence in you and your organization. Authored by Susan Keane Baker and Leslie Bank.

101 Answers to Questions Leaders Ask—By Quint Studer and Studer Group coaches, offers practical, prescriptive solutions to some of the many questions he's received from healthcare leaders around the country.

Over Our Heads: An Analogy on Healthcare, Good Intentions, and Unforeseen Consequences—This book, written by Rulon F. Stacey, PhD, FACHE, uses a grocery store analogy to illustrate how government intervention leads to economic crisis and eventually, collapse.

Nurse Leaders and Nurses
The Nurse Leader Handbook: The Art and Science of Nurse Leadership—By Studer Group senior nursing and physician leaders from across the country, is filled with knowledge that provides nurse leaders with a solid foundation for success. It also serves as a reference they can revisit again and again when they have questions or need a quick refresher course in a particular area of the job.

Inspired Nurse and Inspired Journal—By Rich Bluni, RN, helps maintain and recapture the inspiration nurses felt at the start of their journey with action-oriented "spiritual stretches" and stories that illuminate those sacred moments we all experience.

Emergency Department Team
Excellence in the Emergency Department—A book by Stephanie Baker, RN, CEN, MBA, is filled with proven, easy-to-

implement, step-by-step instructions that will help you move your Emergency Department forward.

For more information about books and other resources, visit www.firestarterpublishing.com.

INSIGHTS FROM STUDER GROUP EXPERTS:

Quick, to-the-point articles from founder Quint Studer and other Studer Group experts provide critical information and incisive commentary on hot industry issues.

To read the latest Insights, as well as archived editions, visit www.studergroup.com.

SOFTWARE SOLUTIONS:

<u>Leader Evaluation Manager</u>^{TM}<u>: Results through Focus and Accountability</u>—Organizations need a way to align goals for their leaders, create a sense of urgency around the most important ones, and hold leaders accountable for meeting their targets. Value-based purchasing, which forces you to improve faster and faster, makes this more critical than ever. Studer Group's Leader Evaluation Manager automates the goal

setting and performance review process for all leaders, creating an aligned organization where everyone is striving for clear, measurable, weighted goals.

Patient Call Manager: The Clinical Call System[SM]—This agile, HIPAA-compliant system—designed to streamline the pre-visit and post-visit call process—allows you to provide a strong continuum of patient care and position your organization to greatly decrease preventable readmissions. It enables users to modify questions by patient risk groupings, focus in on key initiatives, and expand as imposed regulations grow.

To learn more, please visit www.firestarterpublishing.com.

INSTITUTES:

Taking You and Your Organization to the Next Level
At this two-day institute, leaders learn tactics proven to help them quickly move results in the most critical areas: HCAHPS, Core Measures, preventable readmissions, hospital-acquired conditions, and more. They walk away with a clear action plan that yields measurable improvement within 90 days. Even more important, they learn how to implement these tactics in the context of our Evidence-Based Leadership

framework so they can execute quickly and consistently and sustain the results over time.

Excellence in the Emergency Department: Hardwiring Flow & Patient Experience

Crowded Emergency Departments and long patient wait times are no longer acceptable, especially with public reporting of data in the near future. We can predict with great accuracy when lulls and peak times will be, and we know exactly how to improve flow and provide better quality care. This institute will reveal a few simple, hard-hitting tactics that solve the most pressing ED problems *and* create better clinical quality and patient perception of care throughout the entire hospital stay.

Practicing Excellence: Engaging Physicians to Execute System Performance

The changes mandated by health reform make it clear: There will surely be some sort of "marriage" between hospitals and physicians. Regardless of what form it takes, we must start laying the groundwork for a rewarding partnership *now*. Learn our comprehensive methodology for getting physicians aligned with, engaged in, and committed to your organization so that everyone is working together to provide the best possible clinical care, improve HCAHPS results, increase patient loyalty, and gain market share.

What's Right in Health Care®

One of the largest healthcare peer-to-peer learning conferences in the nation, What's Right in Health Care brings organizations together to share ideas that have been proven to make healthcare better. Thousands of leaders attend this institute every year to network with their peers, to hear top industry experts speak, and to learn tactical best practices that allow them to accelerate and sustain performance.

To review a listing of Studer Group institutes or to register for an institute, visit www.studergroup.com/institutes.

For information on Continuing Education Credits, visit www.studergroup.com/cmecredits.

Acknowledgments

My heartfelt thanks to the following:

Quint Studer, who by promising me that he would publish my first book has helped me become something that has truly surprised me: an author! His mentorship continues through his leadership and guidance, his friendship and support. I didn't know it when we first met back in 1986, but I certainly know it now; I was very lucky the day I met Quint!

Mark Clement, Coletta Neuens, and all the leaders who overlooked my flaws, mistakes, and imperfections and had the patience to prepare me to be a leader.

BG Porter for demonstrating that leadership does not need to be loud. He has the remarkable ability to lead with grace, honesty, and kindness. I very much value all of his support at Studer Group.

Mark Albarian for being my best confidant, for listening to me for hours on end and then gently pushing me in the right direction. His vision is the reason that I started this part of my career, and his continued encouragement has kept me going for the past 15 years. I am so grateful for a friend who is always there for me and who knows when to push and question as well as when to cheer and support.

Bill Hejna, who still laughs when I walk into a room, just as he did when we were colleagues at Holy Cross Hospital. His insight into healthcare is laudable. Bill is always the person I turn to when I need to flush out an idea, understand a trend, or develop new material. He also is the person I call when a tough week needs to end with a great dinner, fine wine, and a good laugh.

Patti Gomez for being not only the first leader I have personally mentored, but for being the best! Her success is remarkable and I would be a fool to think it had anything to do with me, but I so appreciate her sharing her career with me. I always look forward to hearing what she is up to, bouncing around strategies with her, and applauding her many successes.

Don Dean for letting me tell our stories across the country and bringing me to present at so many great organizations.

Rich Bluni for keeping people in healthcare all over this country and me "Inspired!"

Sheila Martin, who continues to be a great collaborator and wonderful friend.

Bekki Kennedy for her pure excitement about cookies, cupcakes, and, yes, maybe even pie! Her confidence in my writing, along with her encouragement and support, is the reason why there is this second book.

Jamie Stewart and Candace Edwards from Fire Starter Publishing, whose promotion, support, and assistance have made all the difference in the world for me. I pick up a phone and always get an immediate response, instant answer, or quick solution.

Dottie DeHart and her team (Anna Campbell, Ashley Lamb, and Lindsay Miller) for gearing up for book two. It has been such a privilege to work with such a professional team of editors. I appreciate their advice and I am grateful that they "get" me. Any success I have as an author is because of their extraordinary work.

My team at Liz, inc.: Kathleen Collins, for all you do above and beyond just being an outstanding assistant. I am grateful for the numerous things you do for me, not only professionally, but more importantly, personally. It is a great relief to know that you are at home when I am on the road. And Sue DeMatteo, who is quickly becoming indispensable to our team, who, as part of her many surprising talents, made the cupcakes for the photos!

Most importantly, my friends and family, including my nieces and nephews, who I adore, their parents, and all the folks I am lucky to call friends. My sister, Donna, who celebrates my victories as if they were her own. She is my biggest fan and most loyal enthusiast. And of course, my dear, dear husband, Frank. His calmness soothes me, his humor cheers me, his support sustains me, and his love lifts me. I will never be able to express how this quiet, patient man just means the world to me. I will be forever grateful for his love.

ABOUT THE AUTHOR

An internationally renowned speaker, strategist, and author, Liz Jazwiec consistently ranks amongst the best of the best amongst other speakers. She is author of the award-winning book *Eat That Cookie!: Make Workplace Positivity Pay Off...For Individuals, Teams and Organizations* and is the president and founder of Liz, inc. She has shared her passion for leadership, engagement, and service with fans and followers from many different backgrounds and industries.

She's also been a vice president of patient care, Emergency Department director, executive search professional, and organizational development leader. Her work at Holy Cross Hospital is one of the reasons that the organization was recognized for its award-winning patient satisfaction.

Today she uses all her experience and expertise to inspire organizations committed to building a culture where excellence is driven by strong leaders and engaged employees.

Audiences describe Liz's presentations as uplifting, motivational, and fun. They also clearly respect her practical and experience-based style. You're sure to enjoy her creative and viable suggestions for addressing some of the difficult issues facing leaders and their organizations today. You may contact Liz at www.LizJazz.com.

How to Order Additional Copies of

Hey Cupcake!
We Are ALL Leaders

and

Eat That Cookie!
Make Workplace Positivity Pay Off...For
Individuals, Teams and Organizations

Orders may be placed:

Online at:
www.firestarterpublishing.com
www.studergroup.com

By phone at: 866-354-3473

By mail at: Fire Starter Publishing
913 Gulf Breeze Parkway, Suite 6
Gulf Breeze, FL 32561

(Bulk discounts are available.)

Hey Cupcake! and *Eat That Cookie!*
are also available online at www.amazon.com.